ACHIEVE LEVEL 5

SCIENCE

Practice Questions

By **Gerald Page**

RISING STARS

Rising Stars UK Ltd., 76 Farnaby Road, Bromley, BR1 4BH
Website: www.risingstars-uk.com

All facts are correct at time of going to press.

Published 2002

Editorial: Tanya Solomons
Design: Marc Burville-Riley

British Library Cataloguing in Publication Data
A CIP record for this book is available from the British Library.

ISBN 0-9542202-5-0

Printed in Grimsby, UK

Contents

How to use this book

Topic questions

1 A series of questions on all the topics you need to cover for the Science Test, including some questions on Scientific Enquiry. The first few pages cover the harder bits of Level 4 and the rest cover all the content of Level 5.

2 Each topic matches a section in the Achieve Level 5 Science revision book.

3 Each question has space for the answers, which are included at the back of the book.

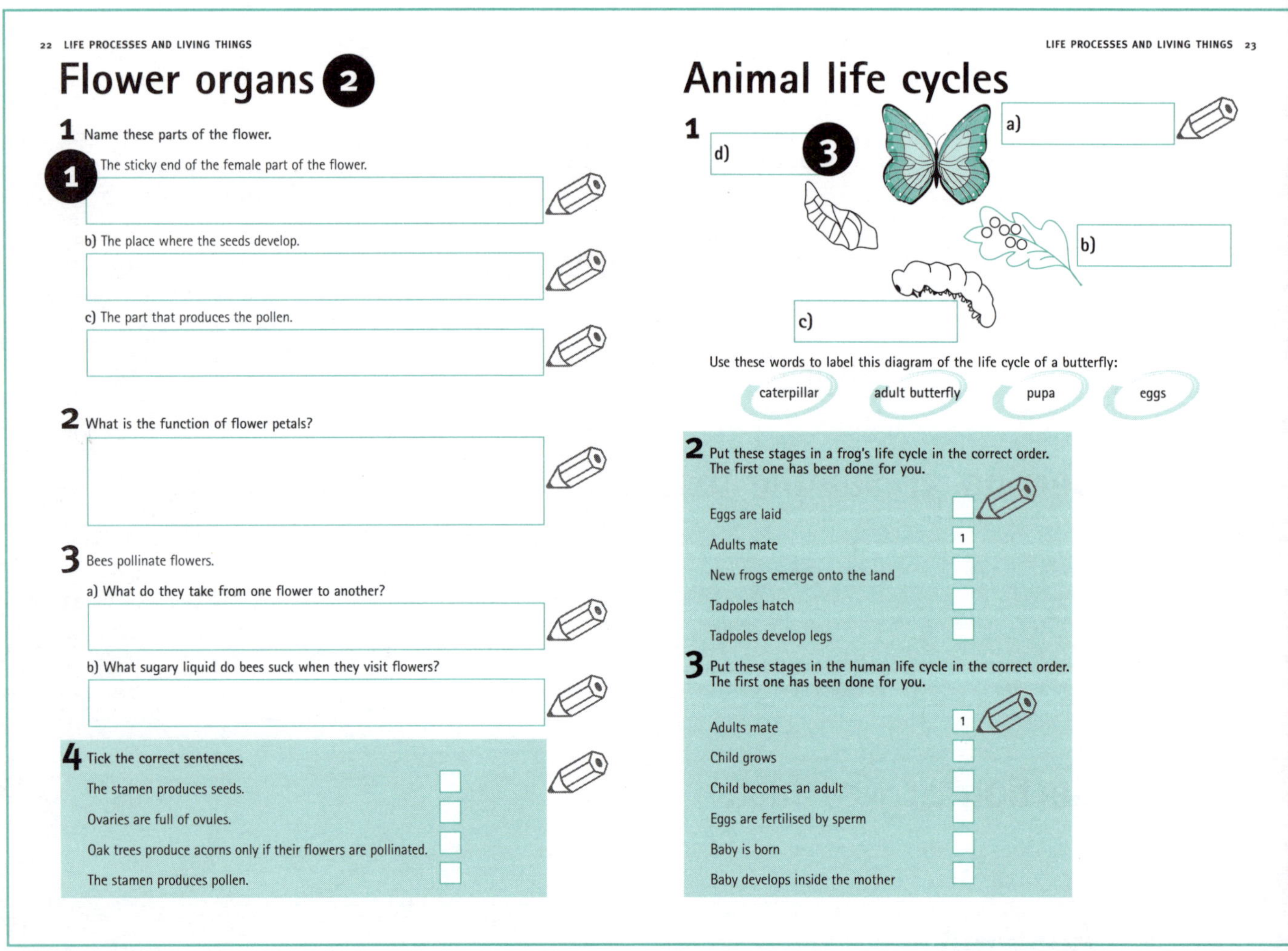

22 LIFE PROCESSES AND LIVING THINGS

Flower organs 2

1 Name these parts of the flower.

1 a) The sticky end of the female part of the flower.

b) The place where the seeds develop.

c) The part that produces the pollen.

2 What is the function of flower petals?

3 Bees pollinate flowers.

a) What do they take from one flower to another?

b) What sugary liquid do bees suck when they visit flowers?

4 Tick the correct sentences.

The stamen produces seeds.

Ovaries are full of ovules.

Oak trees produce acorns only if their flowers are pollinated.

The stamen produces pollen.

LIFE PROCESSES AND LIVING THINGS 23

Animal life cycles

1 d) 3 a) b) c)

Use these words to label this diagram of the life cycle of a butterfly:

caterpillar adult butterfly pupa eggs

2 Put these stages in a frog's life cycle in the correct order. The first one has been done for you.

Eggs are laid

Adults mate 1

New frogs emerge onto the land

Tadpoles hatch

Tadpoles develop legs

3 Put these stages in the human life cycle in the correct order. The first one has been done for you.

Adults mate 1

Child grows

Child becomes an adult

Eggs are fertilised by sperm

Baby is born

Baby develops inside the mother

Level 4 – Sample test

❶ A warm-up test, which practises all the Level 4 Tricky Bits included in the Achieve Level 5 Science revision book.

❷ Each question has space for the answers, which are included at the back of the book.

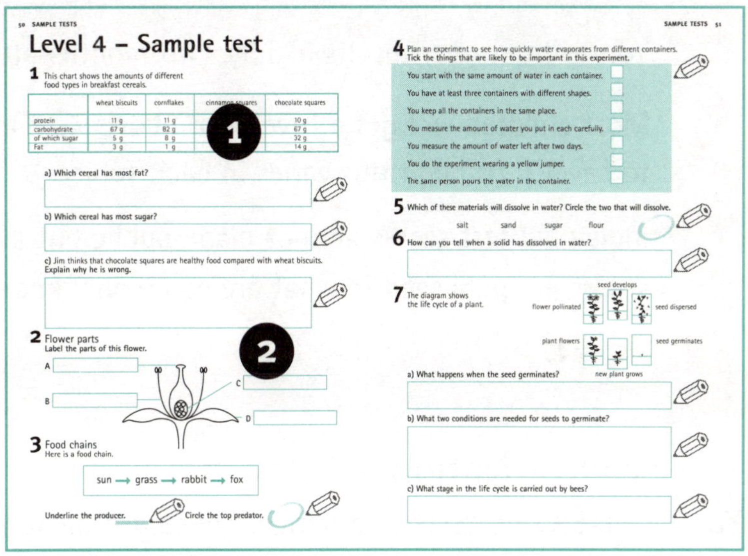

50 SAMPLE TESTS

Level 4 – Sample test

1 This chart shows the amounts of different food types in breakfast cereals.

	wheat biscuits	cornflakes	cinnamon squares	chocolate squares
protein	11 g	11 g		10 g
carbohydrate	67 g	82 g		67 g
of which sugar	5 g	8 g		32 g
Fat	3 g	1 g		14 g

a) Which cereal has most fat?

b) Which cereal has most sugar?

c) Jim thinks that chocolate squares are healthy food compared with wheat biscuits. Explain why he is wrong.

2 Flower parts
Label the parts of this flower.

A B C D

3 Food chains
Here is a food chain.

sun → grass → rabbit → fox

Underline the producer. Circle the top predator.

SAMPLE TESTS 51

4 Plan an experiment to see how quickly water evaporates from different containers. Tick the things that are likely to be important in this experiment.

You start with the same amount of water in each container.
You have at least three containers with different shapes.
You keep all the containers in the same place.
You measure the amount of water you put in each carefully.
You measure the amount of water left after two days.
You do the experiment wearing a yellow jumper.
The same person pours the water in the container.

5 Which of these materials will dissolve in water? Circle the two that will dissolve.

salt sand sugar flour

6 How can you tell when a solid has dissolved in water?

7 The diagram shows the life cycle of a plant.

seed develops, flower pollinated, seed dispersed, plant flowers, seed germinates, new plant grows

a) What happens when the seed germinates?

b) What two conditions are needed for seeds to germinate?

c) What stage in the life cycle is carried out by bees?

Level 5 – Sample test

❶ A final test covering all the Level 5 content, which allows you to see which areas you have got to grips with and which areas you still need to revise. The sample test is similar to the real SATs, as it starts with some easy questions and gets harder as the test goes on.

❷ Each question has space for the answers, which are included at the back of the book.

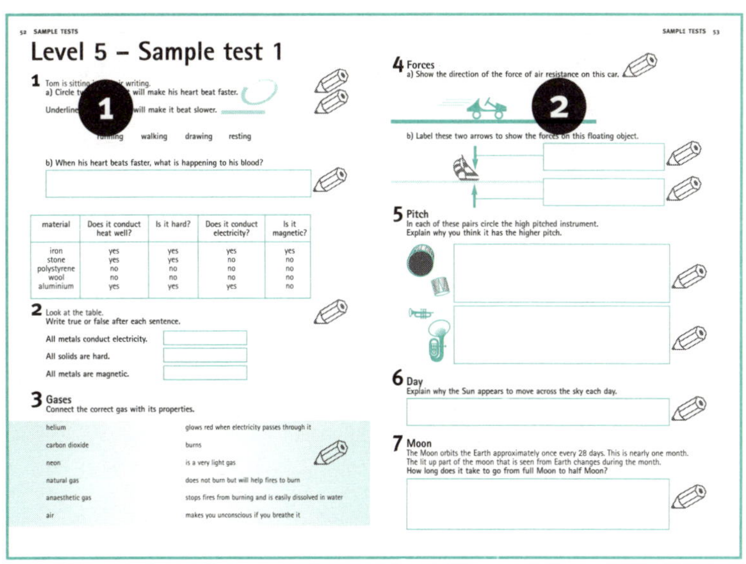

52 SAMPLE TESTS

Level 5 – Sample test 1

1 Tom is sitting … writing.
a) Circle … will make his heart beat faster.
Underline … will make it beat slower.

running walking drawing resting

b) When his heart beats faster, what is happening to his blood?

material	Does it conduct heat well?	Is it hard?	Does it conduct electricity?	Is it magnetic?
iron	yes	yes	yes	yes
stone	yes	yes	no	no
polystyrene	no	no	no	no
wool	no	no	no	no
aluminium	yes	yes	yes	no

2 Look at the table.
Write true or false after each sentence.

All metals conduct electricity.
All solids are hard.
All metals are magnetic.

3 Gases
Connect the correct gas with its properties.

helium	glows red when electricity passes through it
carbon dioxide	burns
neon	is a very light gas
natural gas	does not burn but will help fires to burn
anaesthetic gas	stops fires from burning and is easily dissolved in water
air	makes you unconscious if you breathe it

SAMPLE TESTS 53

4 Forces
a) Show the direction of the force of air resistance on this car.

b) Label these two arrows to show the forces on this floating object.

5 Pitch
In each of these pairs circle the high pitched instrument.
Explain why you think it has the higher pitch.

6 Day
Explain why the Sun appears to move across the sky each day.

7 Moon
The Moon orbits the Earth approximately once every 28 days. This is nearly one month.
The lit up part of the moon that is seen from Earth changes during the month.
How long does it take to go from full Moon to half Moon?

The 2003 SATs

Key Facts

- The Key Stage 2 National Tests (or SATs) take place in the middle of May in Year 6. You will be tested on Maths, English and Science.
- The tests take place in your school and will be marked by examiners – not your teacher!
- You will get your results in July, two months after you take the tests.
- Most children will get a Level 4 or above with about 30% getting to Level 5 (though this varies in each subject).
- Individual test scores are not made public but a school's combined scores are published in what are commonly known as league tables.

The Science National Tests

You will take two tests in Science. These are designed to test your knowledge and skills across the following areas of Science:

- Life processes and living things – the human body, plants and animals.
- Materials and their properties – changing different materials, understanding the characteristics of different materials.
- Physical processes – electricity, forces, light and sound, the Sun and the Earth.

STOP PRESS

Scientific Enquiry – There will be more questions testing your skills of scientific enquiry in 2003 than in previous years. These will include selecting the correct approach in an investigation and carrying it out effectively by selecting the right equipment; making the correct observations or measurements and recording your results systematically; and using scientific language and data handling skills. Don't worry – you won't have to carry out an actual investigation but you might have to think about one that is described to you and answer questions about it.

Many of the questions include elements of scientific enquiry but we have also added extra pages with specific questions designed to help you succeed in this new area of testing:
pages 17–19, pages 48–49 and pages 55–56

The Science Tests

There will be two Science Tests each one lasting approximately 45 minutes.

ACHIEVE LEVEL 5

Test tips and technique

Before the test

1. When you revise, try revising a 'little and often' rather than in long sessions.
2. Learn the Key Facts (at the end of the book) so that you can recall them instantly. These are your tools for performing your calculations.
3. Revise with a friend. You can encourage and learn from each other.
4. Get a good night's sleep the night before.
5. Make sure you have breakfast!
6. Be prepared – bring your own pens and pencils and wear a watch to check the time as you go.

During the test

1. Don't rush the first few questions. These tend to be quite straightforward, so don't make any silly mistakes.
2. As you know by now, READ THE QUESTION THEN READ IT AGAIN.
3. If you get stuck, don't linger on the same question – move on! You can come back to it later.
4. Never leave a multiple choice question. Guess if you really can't work out the answer.
5. Check to see how many marks a question is worth. Have you 'earned' those marks with your answer?
6. Check your answers after each question. Does your answer look correct?
7. Be aware of the time. After 20 minutes, check to see how far you have got.

8 Try to leave a couple of minutes at the end to read through what you have written.

9 Always show your working out. You may get a mark for showing you have gone through the correct procedure even if your answer is wrong.

10 Don't leave any questions unanswered. In the two minutes you have left yourself at the end, make an educated guess at the questions you really couldn't do.

11 Remember, as long as you have done your best, nobody can ask for more. Only you will know if that is the case. Good luck!

Things to remember

1 Don't panic! If you see a difficult question, take your time, re-read it and have a go!

2 Check every question and every page to be sure you don't miss any! Some questions will want two answers.

3 If a question is about measuring, always write in the UNIT of MEASUREMENT (e.g. newtons, l, kg).

4 Don't be afraid to ask a teacher for anything you need, such as tracing paper or another pencil.

5 Write neatly – if you want to change an answer, put a line through it and write beside the answer box.

6 Always double-check your answers.

Roots and stems

1 **Put a tick next to the sentences that are true.**

Stems anchor the plant in the soil. ☐

Water travels up stems to leaves. ☐

Stems hold the leaves and flowers above the soil. ☐

Roots make food for plants. ☐

2 The Baobab tree grows in parts of Africa where there is little rainfall.
Its roots reach deep down into the soil and its trunk is hollow.

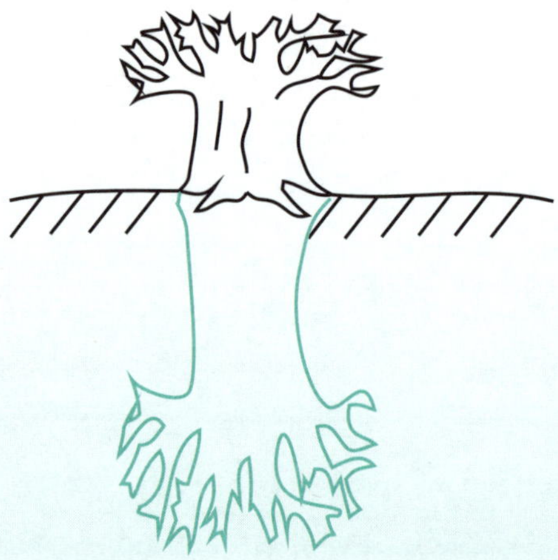

Explain how the baobab tree is adapted to its habitat.

3 When companies dig up the road to put in pipes and cables they must be careful when digging near trees.
Give two reasons why they should be careful.

a)

b)

4 Water travels up the trunk of a tree just below the bark.
Trees die if a ring of bark is removed.
Why does this happen?
Use these words in your answer: roots water leaves

Flower parts

1 Label this diagram of a flower using these words: stigma ovary petal stamen

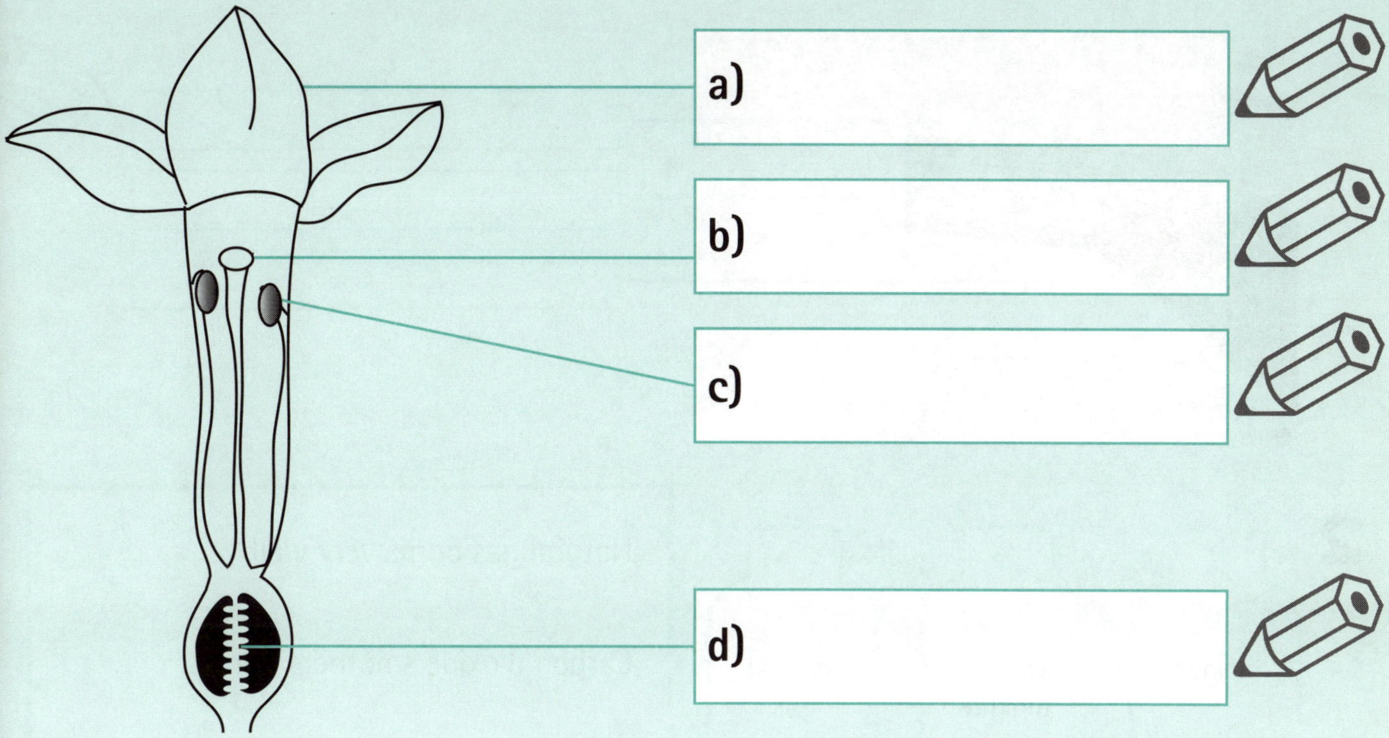

2 Label this diagram of a flower.

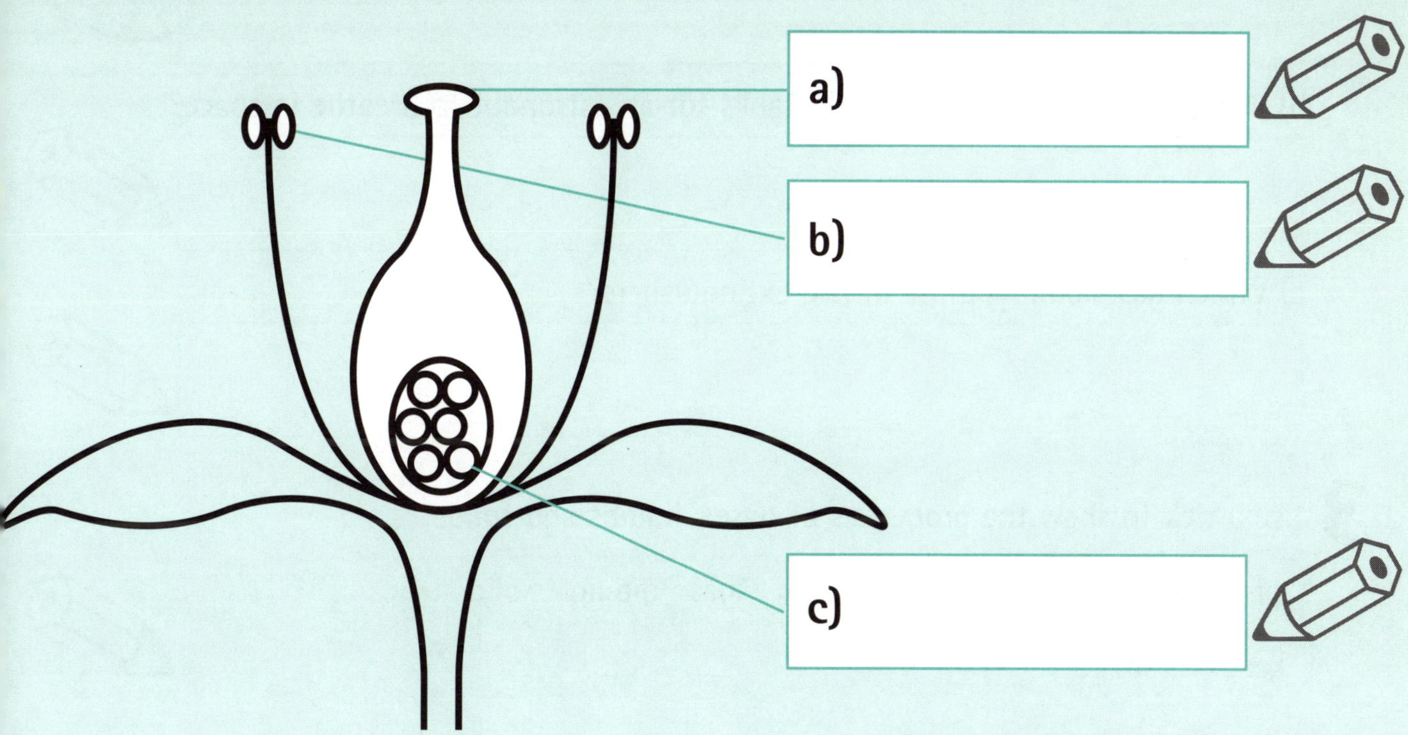

Gases

1 Label this diagram using these words: carbon dioxide air natural gas

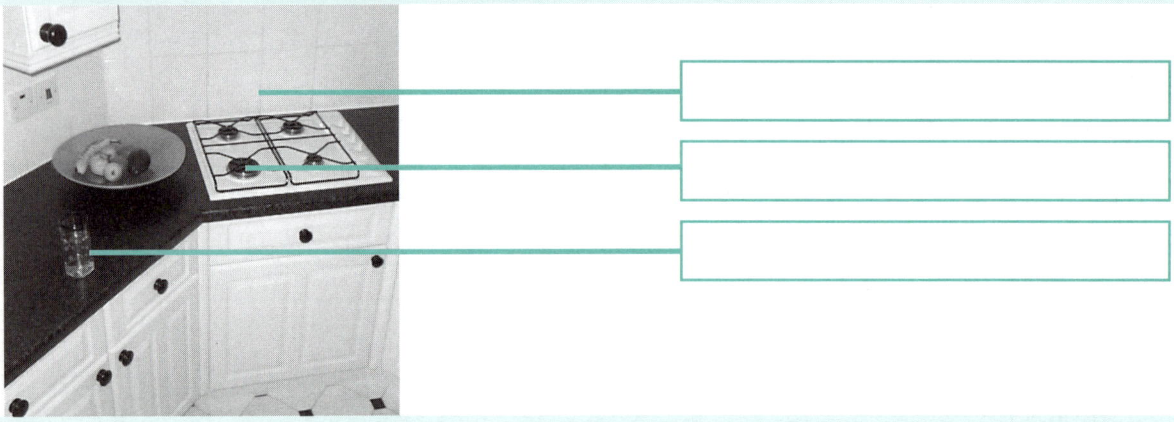

2

Natural gas burns very well.

Carbon dioxide smothers flames.

Oxygen is a part of the air we breathe.

a) Which gas would you connect to a stove to heat food?

b) Which gas would you use to fill tanks for an astronaut to breathe in space?

c) Which gas would you use in fire extinguishers?

3 Use a tick to show the properties of gases, liquids and solids

property	gas	liquid	solid
keeps its shape			
flows through a pipe			
can be squashed into a small space			

Separating mixtures

1 Matt dissolves some sugar in water.

Explain how he could get the sugar back.

2 Pat wants to make some muddy water clear.

Explain how he could do this.

3 Jim has a mixture of tiny aluminium pins and tiny iron pins.
They are the same size and shape.

What is the easiest way to separate them?

4 Kate has a mixture of polystyrene beads and small ball bearings.
Both are the same size.

**Apart from picking them out one at a time,
what is the easiest way to separate this mixture?**

Forces

1 a) Jim slides on the snow.
What are the forces that slow him down?

b) Jim drags the toboggan along the flat ground.
Draw an arrow to show the direction of friction.

2 Explain why walking boots need a patterned sole.
What is the force they are using to stop them slipping?

3 Sharon sits on a slide. It isn't very slippery. She doesn't move.
Tick the two correct sentences.

Friction is stopping her from sliding. ☐

Gravity is stopping her sliding. ☐

Gravity is not working. ☐

Friction force is working against gravity. ☐

4 Jan is on her bike. She rolls down a hill. She uses her brakes to stop her.

a) What force pulls her downhill?

b) What force does she use to stop the bike?

Magnets

1 Rajiv is exploring the way magnets attract and repel.
Write what will happen when he brings the different ends of the magnets together.

a) He brings the north pole of one magnet near the north pole of the other magnet.

The magnets ______ **each other.**

b) He brings the north pole of one magnet near the south pole of the other magnet.

The magnets ______ **each other.**

c) He brings the south pole of one magnet near the north pole of the other magnet.

The magnets ______ **each other.**

d) He brings the south pole of one magnet near the south pole of the other magnet.

The magnets ______ **each other.**

2 Pete is testing coins with a magnet.
He finds some are attracted to the magnets and others are not.
What do you think the coins that are attracted are made from?

3 **a) Naima thinks that all metals are attracted to magnets. Is she right?**

b) Explain your answer.

4 Naima wonders if magnetism passes through paper.
What simple test can she do to find out?

Sorting materials

1 Jane investigated the properties of materials.
Complete the table. The first row has been done for you.

Material	attracted to magnet	transparent	opaque	waterproof	conducts electricity
pottery	no	no	yes	yes	no
steel					
gold					
window glass					
rock					

2 Finish each sentence below.

a) I know that a pencil is a solid because

b) I know that shampoo is a liquid because

c) I know that natural gas is a gas because

3 Kim heated different materials on a spoon in a candle flame.
Draw a line to connect the material with what happened.

sugar	nothing happened
water	it melted
butter	it bubbled and turned black
salt	it boiled and evaporated

4 Water is found in many forms.
Write whether each of these is a solid, a liquid or a gas.

rain

snow

fog

clouds

ice

Scientific enquiry

1 Tim is investigating rocks. He lists some questions.
Tick the questions that would be easy to answer using tests done in the classroom.

Which rocks soak up water? ☐

How are rocks made? ☐

Which rocks are hard and which rocks are soft? ☐

Which rocks have crystals in them and which do not? ☐

Why do some rocks have fossils and others not? ☐

How old are rocks? ☐

2 He finds that two rocks soak up water.
He wants to find which of the two soak up most water.
List the stages in his investigation.

a) He starts by weighing the two dry rocks.

b)

c)

3 After the experiment he wants to check their dry weight.
What will he have to do?

4 **Which of these rocks do you think would burn?**

granite ☐

coal ☐

sandstone ☐

Scientific enquiry – handling data

1 Sam puts a damp pot plant on some scales.
He checks its weight over six days.
He draws a graph of results.

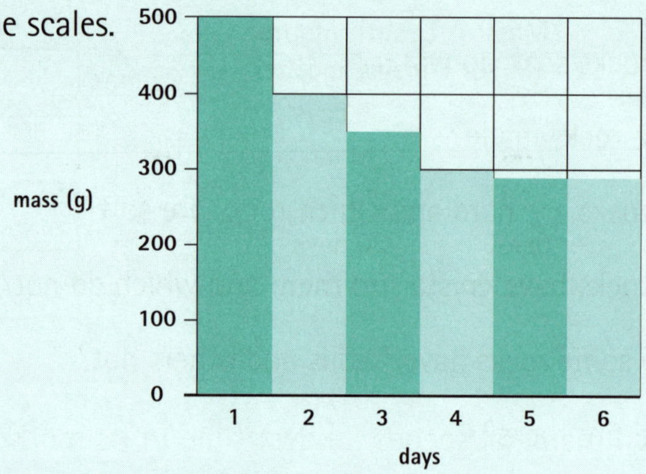

a) What is the mass of the pot plant at the start of the experiment?

b) What is the mass of the dry pot plant?

c) Tick the day on which the pot plant dried out most.

first day ☐ fourth day ☐

second day ☐ fifth day ☐

third day ☐ sixth day ☐

2 This table shows the distance that a ball rolled off a ramp.

height of ramp	1	2	3	4	5
distance ball rolled	21	32	43	54	?

a) What happened to the distance as the ramp got higher?

The experiment was not done with the ramp at height 5.
b) Predict the distance the ball might travel.

3 This table shows the mass of an adult and the time a baby spends inside its mother before birth.

a) Use the data to complete this bar chart.

Name of mammal	Mass (kg)	Length of time inside mother
Cat	2	65 days
Chimp	60	210 days
Human	80	270 days
Mouse	0.005	20 days
Lion	150	110 days

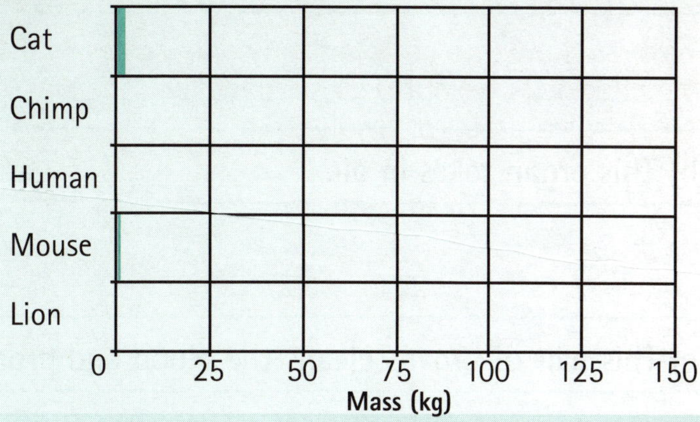

b) Which mammal spends longest time in its mother?

c) Which mammal spends shortest time in its mother?

d) Which mammal is heaviest?

e) Which mammal has the smallest mass?

f) What is the connection between the weight of a mammal and the time it spends inside its mother?

g) Put a tick next to the sentences that are true.

Lions spend more time inside their mother's body than cats. ☐

Mice are very small and spend a long time inside their mother's body. ☐

Big mammals spend longer inside their mother's body than small ones. ☐

Chimps weigh more than humans. ☐

Humans spend longest inside their mother's body so they can develop a big brain. ☐

Human organs

1 Name these organs.

a) This organ controls your movement and thinking.

b) This organ takes in air.

c) This pair of organs cleans the blood and produces urine.

d) This organ breaks up food and starts digestion.

2 The heart pumps blood around the body.
This diagram shows the path of the blood.

Use a red pen or pencil to trace the path of the blood that carries oxygen.

Use a blue pen or pencil to trace the path of the blood that does not carry oxygen.

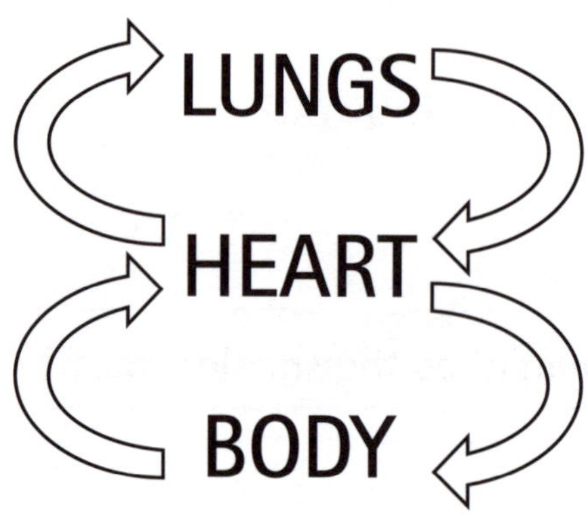

3 What is the name of the blood vessels that carry blood away from the heart?

4 What is the name of the blood vessels that carry blood back to the heart?

5 What is the name of the tiny blood vessels that bleed if you cut your finger?

Pulse rate and the heart

1 The heart pumps blood around the body.
Name two things that blood carries around the body.

2 Exercise makes the heart beat faster.
Why does this happen?

3 Liam was attached to a heart rate monitor. The number of beats per minute was recorded.
a) Complete the table.

activity	before activity	during the activity	after resting for 15 minutes
watching TV	80	80	80
walking slowly	80	110	
jogging			
running fast		140	

b) Explain how you decided on the number of heartbeats when jogging.

4 This line graph shows Dan's pulse rate during half an hour.
During the half hour Dan was

walking
resting
running

What do you think Dan was doing at points A, B and C?

A

B

C

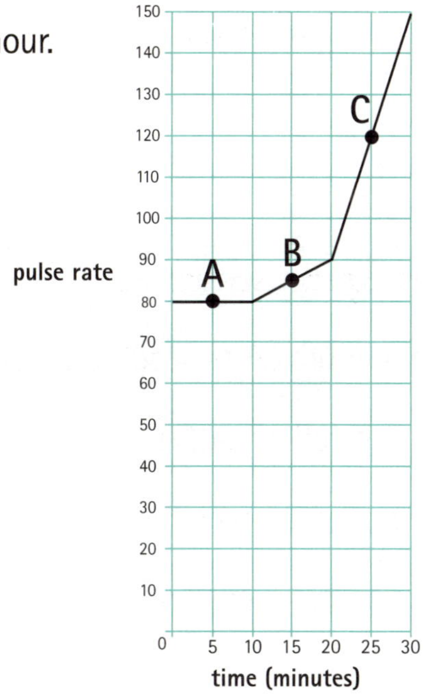

Flower organs

1 Name these parts of the flower.

a) The sticky end of the female part of the flower.

b) The place where the seeds develop.

c) The part that produces the pollen.

2 What is the function of flower petals?

3 Bees pollinate flowers.

a) What do they take from one flower to another?

b) What sugary liquid do bees suck when they visit flowers?

4 Tick the correct sentences.

The stamen produces seeds. ☐

Ovaries are full of ovules. ☐

Oak trees produce acorns only if their flowers are pollinated. ☐

The stamen produces pollen. ☐

Animal life cycles

1

Use these words to label this diagram of the life cycle of a butterfly:

caterpillar adult butterfly pupa eggs

2 Put these stages in a frog's life cycle in the correct order. The first one has been done for you.

Eggs are laid	
Adults mate	1
New frogs emerge onto the land	
Tadpoles hatch	
Tadpoles develop legs	

3 Put these stages in the human life cycle in the correct order. The first one has been done for you.

Adults mate	1
Child grows	
Child becomes an adult	
Eggs are fertilised by sperm	
Baby is born	
Baby develops inside the mother	

Plant life cycles

1 Here are the stages in a flowering plant's life cycle.
They are in the wrong order.

a new plant grows
b seed germinates
c seed develops
d plant flowers
e seed dispersed
f flower pollinated

Write the letters in the correct order in this life cycle:

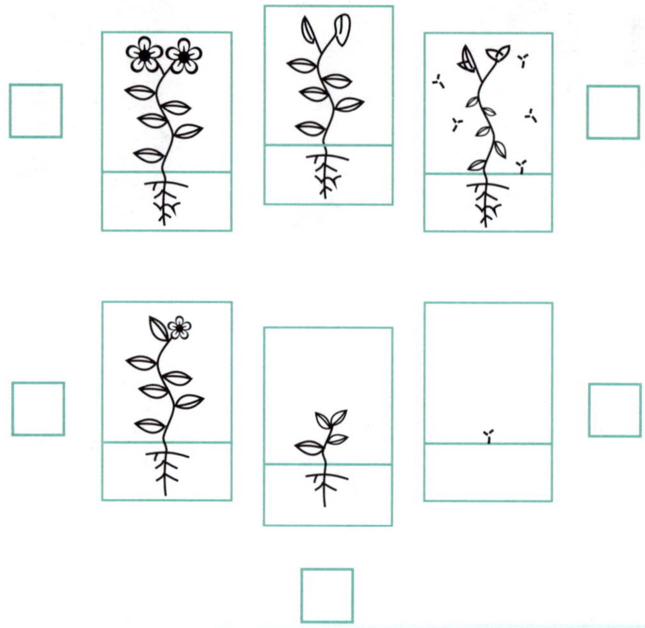

2 Seeds are spread in a number of ways.
Draw a line from the seed to the way it is spread.

apple seeds	float in the sea to other islands
acorns	eaten by animals such as pigs and carried in droppings
sycamore seeds	blown by the wind
coconut seeds	buried by squirrels and then forgotten

3 **Explain why seeds need to be moved away from the parent plant.**

4 **What three things does a seed need to germinate?**

5 **What three things does a plant need to grow?**

Keys and classifying

1 Use the key to identify the animals below.

A

B

Does it have wings?

yes

Is it covered with feathers?

yes — nightjar

no — pipistrelle

no

Does it have a furry tail?

yes — polecat

no — watervole

A is ______

B is ______

2 Write these animals in the correct boxes.

spider

insect

amphibian

reptile

Does it have a backbone?

yes

Is it covered with scales?

yes ______

no ______

no

Does it have six legs?

yes ______

no ______

Habitats

1 Plants live in places that suit them best.

Draw a line to match the plant to the environment where it grows.

cactus	on walls
moss	in hot deserts
reeds	in short grass
bluebells	in very damp places
daisies	under deciduous trees

2 The children set up an experiment. They put snails in a tank.
They put different things in each corner:

damp paper	dry paper	damp paper and lettuce leaves	damp paper and lettuce leaves under an upturned box

They counted the number of snails in each corner:

damp paper	dry paper	damp paper and lettuce leaves	damp paper and lettuce leaves under an upturned box
0 snails	0 snails	3 snails	12 snails

a) Which habitat did the snails prefer?

b) Explain why they preferred this habitat. Give three reasons.

3 Some moss is growing on a brick wall in a sunny place.
What problems does moss have in this habitat?
Write two sentences. Use one of these words in each sentence.

soil

water

Adaptation to the environment

1 Seals are adapted to life in the water because they have:
• a streamlined shape • a layer of blubber to keep them warm • sharp teeth to catch fish

List the ways in which penguins are adapted to life in the sea.

2 Finish these sentences about the ways in which polar bears are adapted to life on the ice.

a) Polar bears are ______ to camouflage them against the ice.

b) Polar bears have ______ to insulate them against the cold.

c) Polar bears have massive claws ______

3 Which part of a blackberry bush helps stop animals from eating it?

4 Which part of a hedgehog's body helps stop foxes from eating it?

5 Draw a line to match the adaptation to each animal or plant.

antelope	very large claws and teeth
lion	big front feet to dig through the soil
camel	very fast runner and good hearing
owl	huge ears to catch echoes at night
bat	huge eyes to see at night
mole	long root to get at water
dandelion	humps in which to store fat

Classification

1 Draw a line to match the type of animal to its description.

fish	feeds young on milk
amphibian	lays eggs with a hard shell
reptile	has fins
bird	has a dry scaly skin
mammal	can live on land but lays eggs in water

2 Name one example of each of these animal groups:

fish

amphibian

reptile

bird

mammal

3 Fran was looking in rock pools by the sea. She found types of plants and animals:

Write these words in the empty boxes below:

starfish   fish   sea anemones   seaweed

Living things Fran found

Does it have fins?

yes   no

Does it have five arms?

yes   no

Does it catch small animals with its tentacles?

yes   no

Competition

1 Two sycamore tree seedlings are growing near the parent tree.
One is growing directly under the branches of the parent tree.
The other is growing in the open away from the tree.

a) Which seedling do you expect to grow best?

b) Give two reasons for your answer

2 Jim sows fifty seeds in a small plant pot of compost.
All the seeds germinate. There is only room for three plants in the pot.

a) What eventually happens to all the other seedlings?

b) Explain why this happens

3 Some children were talking about lions.
On the African grasslands lions are the strongest predators. Nothing eats lions.
So why are there only a few lions?
Jim thinks it is because lions do not breed quickly.
Kay thinks it is because there is a limited amount of food.
Lenny thinks it is because lions spread out into other places.

Why do you think that the lion population does not increase all the time?

Burning

1 Paul heated some materials in a candle flame.
He made a table of results.
Fill in the table for bread and aluminium foil.

material	appearance before heating	what happened after 20 seconds in the flame	what happened after 2 minutes in the flame
wax	white, translucent solid	melted and went transparent	began to burn
sugar	white powder	melted	turned into a black solid
pebble	grey stone	nothing	nothing
cotton	red soft material	began to go brown	burnt and ended up as ash
nylon	green, shiny	began to melt and bubble	burnt and turned into a black solid
bread			
aluminium foil			

2 Which materials melted?

3 Name another material that would melt in a candle flame.

4 Which materials burned?

5 Name another material that will burn if put into a candle flame.

Mixtures

1 a) When a solid is dissolved in water, what is the mixture called?

b) Circle the word that describes a solid that will not dissolve in water.

undissolved   not mixed   insoluble

2 Give two ways you know that a solid has dissolved and not just mixed in with water.

3 Harry investigated the speed at which sugar dissolved in water.
Tick the things that made the sugar dissolve more quickly.

Using warm water	☐
Using a container made of glass	☐
Stirring the water	☐
Using cold water	☐
Putting the mixture in the light	☐

4 Rajiv investigated the speed at which different types of sugar dissolved in water.
He used: Big crystals   Medium grains   Fine grains

a) Write three things he should keep the same for each of the sugars.

b) Which sugar do you think will dissolve most quickly?

c) Explain your answer.

Evaporation

1 **Tick the correct box.**
Evaporation is the change from

solid to liquid ☐

solid to gas ☐

liquid to gas ☐

2 Some children did a test to see how quickly water evaporated in different places.
They put the same amount of water in the same sort of container.

They put the three containers in different places:
A on a warm radiator **B** in a cool cupboard **C** in a warm room

a) Explain why the water in A evaporated quickest.

b) Explain why the water in B evaporated slowest.

3 Joe and Jill put 100 ml of water in three jars.
Jar **A** had the lid firmly screwed on
Jar **B** had the lid resting on the top
Jar **C** had the lid taken off

a) Complete the table with the letters of the correct jars.

jar (letter)	**amount left in jar after two days**
	100 ml
	15 ml
	95 ml

b) Explain why one of the jars did not evaporate at all.

Liquids and gases

1 Kim puts ice into a glass of water.
After a minute small drops of water appear on the outside of the glass.
What is the process causing these drops to form?

2 Mike is having a hot bath. He notices the mirror in the bathroom is misty.
a) What is the liquid that makes the mirror misty?

b) Where does this liquid come from?

3 Sam's dad puts a lid on a boiling pan. He says it stops the windows misting over.
a) Is he right?

b) Explain your answer.

4 Faye puts the same amount of water in three cans.
She puts: ice and water in one can
warm water in one can
hot water from the tap in one of the cans

She thinks that only the can with ice in will have small drops of water form on the outside.
Explain why she thinks this will happen.

Change of state

1 What are these changes called?

solid → liquid

liquid → gas

liquid → solid

gas → liquid

2 Yasmin put ice cubes into different places. She timed how long they took to melt.

place where ice cube was placed	time taken to melt completely
in some warm water	1 minute
in cold water	4 minutes
on a saucer in the classroom	45 minutes
on a saucer in a fridge	98 minutes

Explain the pattern of these results.

3 David put a plastic beaker of water into the freezer. He put a sensor in the water.

When it came out of the freezer he plugged the sensor into a computer.

It recorded the temperature of the water as it warmed up in the room.

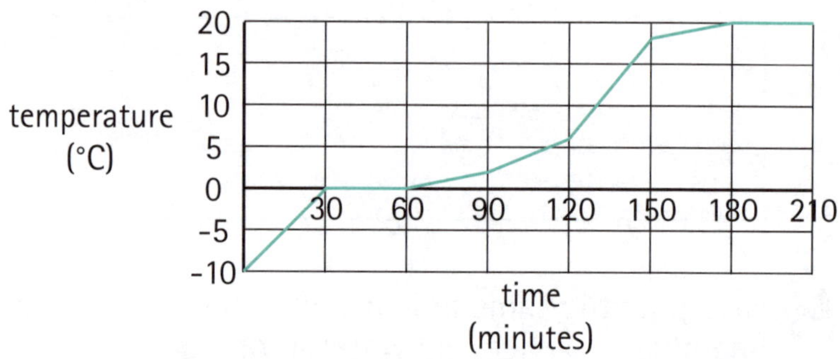

a) What was the temperature inside the freezer?

b) Mark an X on the graph line where there was still solid ice in the beaker.

c) What was the temperature of the air in the room?

Separating materials

1 Sometimes gravy gets lumps in it.

Explain how you separate the lumps from the rest of the gravy.

2 Explain how you could separate a mixture of sugar and water.

3 Explain how you could separate a mixture of sand and salt.

4 Give an example of a mixture you could separate using a magnet.

5 Give an example of a mixture you could separate by letting one of the materials float and the other material sink.

6 Dan poured a mixture of salt, flour and water through a filter paper.
A white sludge was left in the paper.
The water was left to evaporate and a white crystal was left behind.

a) Was the white sludge salt or flour?

b) Were the white crystals salt or flour?

Electricity symbols

1 Label this diagram. Use these words:

- bulb
- wire
- battery

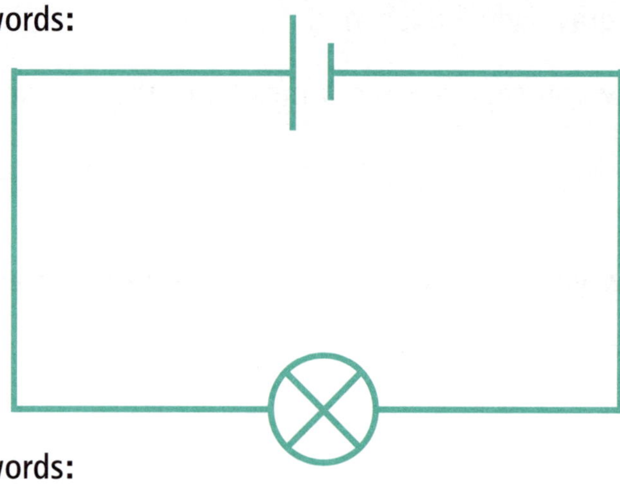

2 Label this diagram. Use these words:

- wire
- battery
- switch
- buzzer

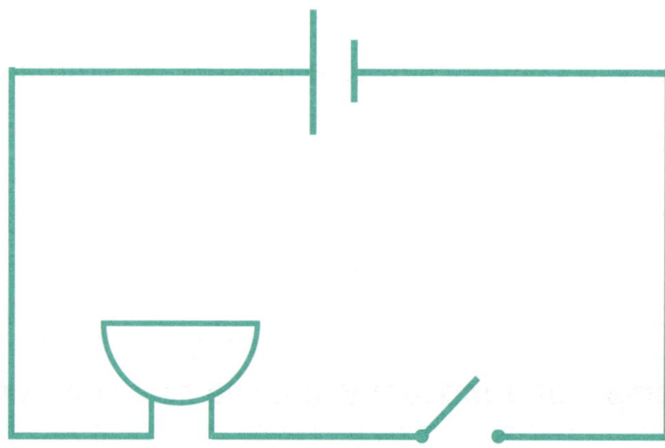

3 What will happen when the switch is closed?

4 Draw a series circuit with three bulbs in series, a closed switch and two batteries.

Changing the flow of electricity

1 In these three circuits the bulbs are identical.
a) Tick the circuit in which the bulb will glow most brightly.

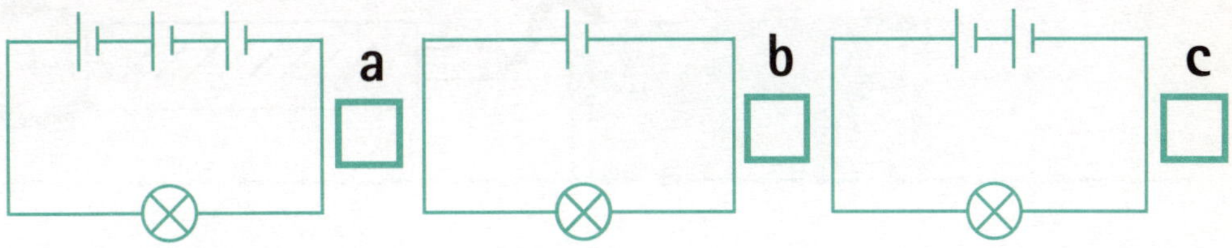

b) Explain why you have ticked that circuit.

2 In these circuits the bulbs and batteries are identical.
Tick the circuit in which the bulb will glow most brightly.

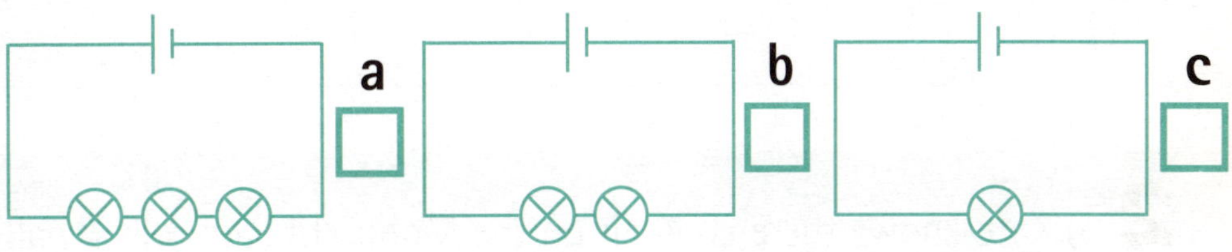

3 In this circuit the electricity runs through the wires, through the bulb and through the pencil lead.
a) What effect does the pencil lead have on the brightness of the bulb?

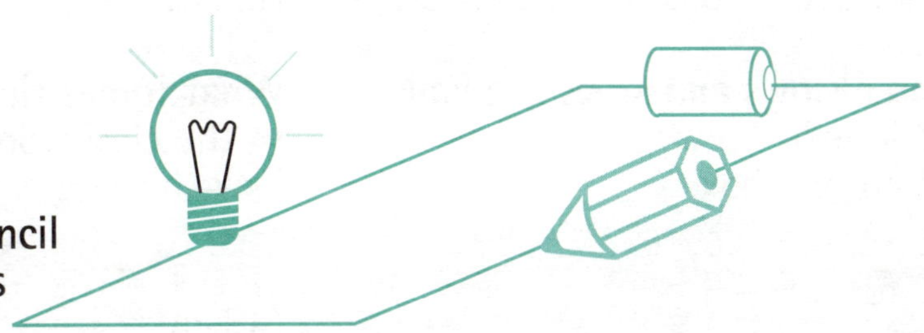

b) What effect does the pencil lead have on the flow of electricity?

4 In this circuit the electricity runs through the wires, through the motor and through the pencil lead.
What effect does the pencil lead have on the speed of the motor?

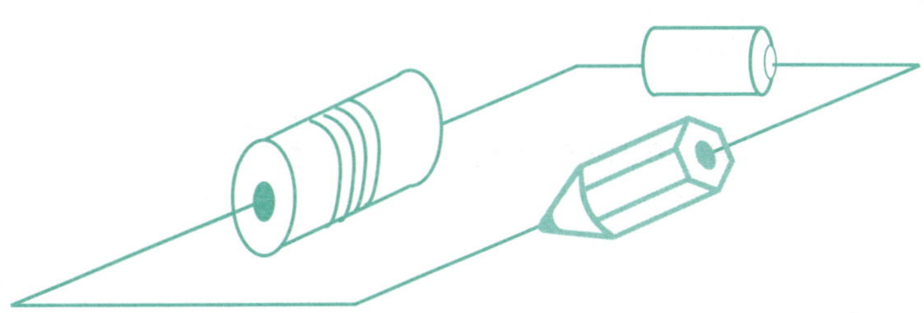

Forces

1

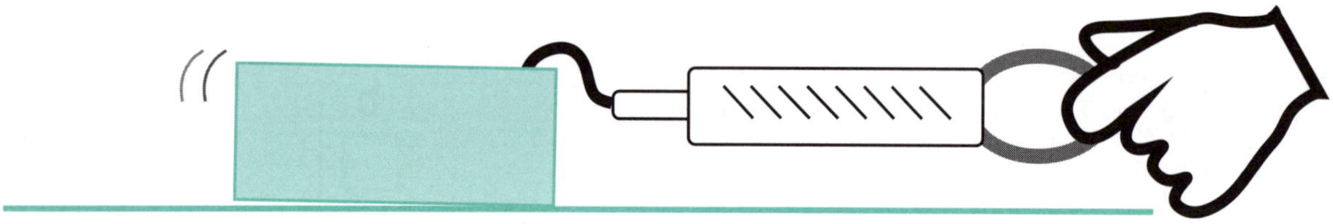

Jim pulls a box along the table top.
He uses a forcemeter to measure the force of his pull.

What is the name of the force that makes it hard to pull the box?

2

a) Kate knows there is no air on the Moon. She sees astronauts rolling a ball on the Moon's surface. It rolls then slowly stops.

What force slows and stops the ball on the Moon?
Tick the correct box.

- Gravity ☐
- Friction ☐
- Dust ☐
- Upthrust ☐
- Air resistance ☐

b) Paul rolls a ball down a ramp in his classroom.
He notices that it slows and stops.

What forces slow and stop the ball in the classroom?
Tick the two correct boxes.

- Gravity ☐
- Friction ☐
- Dust ☐
- Upthrust ☐
- Air resistance ☐

3

It is a snowy day.
Layla slides downhill on a sledge.

What two forces does she want to REDUCE so she slides further?

Forces

1 Dan knows that gravity pulls on masses.
He uses a forcemeter to measure the pull of gravity on different masses.
He shows his results on a line graph.

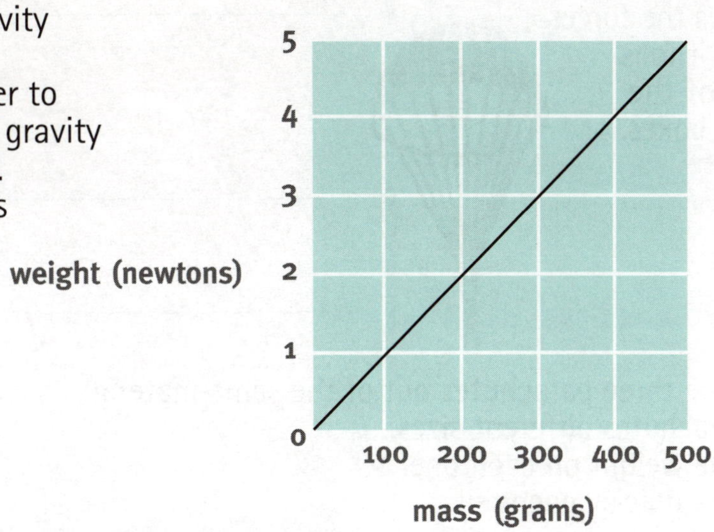

a) What mass had a weight of 3 N?

b) Predict the pull of gravity on a mass of 900 g.

2 Pam drops two balls.
One is a golf ball weighing 100 g. The other is a football weighing 400 g.

She drops them at the same time from the same height.
Tick one answer:

- They will hit the ground at the same time ☐
- The football will hit the ground first ☐
- The golf ball will hit the ground first ☐

Forces

1 This diagram shows the forces on a parachute as it falls.
Write the names of the two forces in the boxes.

2 Some children made three parachutes out of the same material.
They made the parachutes different sizes.
They used the same weight on each one.
They measured how quickly each fell.

parachute	area of parachute canopy	time taken to hit ground
X	200 cm^2	1.2 seconds
Y	400 cm^2	2.0 seconds
Z	800 cm^2	2.3 seconds

Who is correct?

3 Pat thinks that astronauts should use parachutes to land safely on the Moon.

Why is this a bad idea?

Forces

1 Kyle floated a toy boat in a fish tank.
Write the names of the two forces in the boxes.

2 Kyle then weighed a brick using a forcemeter.

He weighed it in air.

He weighed it with the brick in water.

In air the brick weighs 8 N.
In water the brick weighs 6 N.

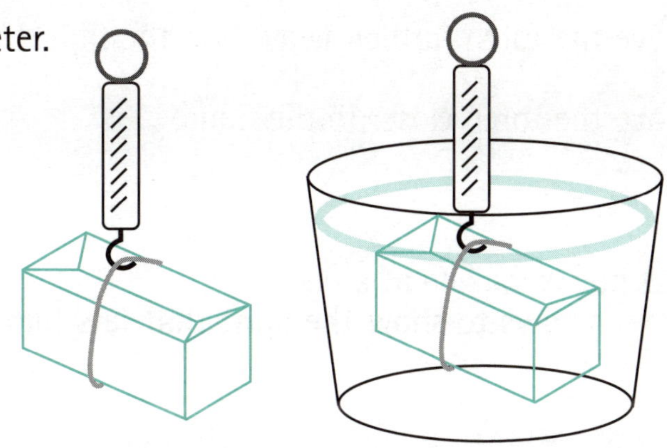

Explain why the brick weighed less in water than in air.

3 At the docks a ship was loaded with wood.
The children talked about what would happen.

Which child is correct?

Shadows

1 Jill is using this torch to make shadows on the paper.
How could she make the size of the shadow bigger?
Tick the two correct boxes.

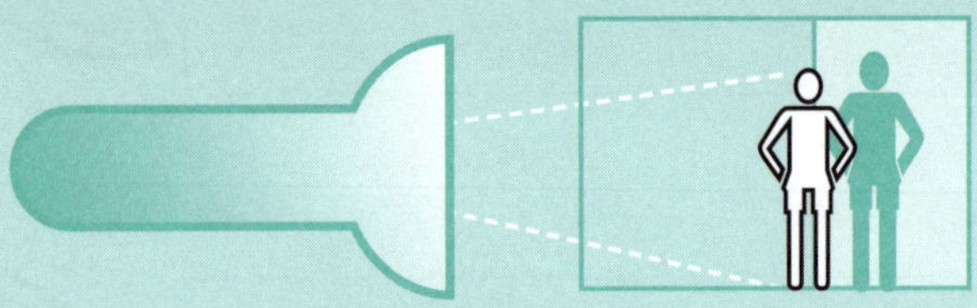

- Move the figure closer to the screen. ☐
- Move the figure closer to the torch. ☐
- Use a brighter torch. ☐
- Move the torch further away from the figure. ☐
- Move the torch closer to the figure. ☐

2 This boy is looking at a book.
Draw arrows to show the light that lets him see the book.

3 Kim and Lee talked about the difference between a reflection and a shadow.
Tick the two correct boxes.

- A reflection happens when light bounces off something. ☐
- A reflection only happens when light bounces off a mirror. ☐
- A shadow happens when light is blocked. ☐
- A shadow happens when light passes through objects. ☐

Reflections

1 Mel and Rita are trying to see the reflection of the TV in the mirror.
a) Who can see the TV in the mirror?

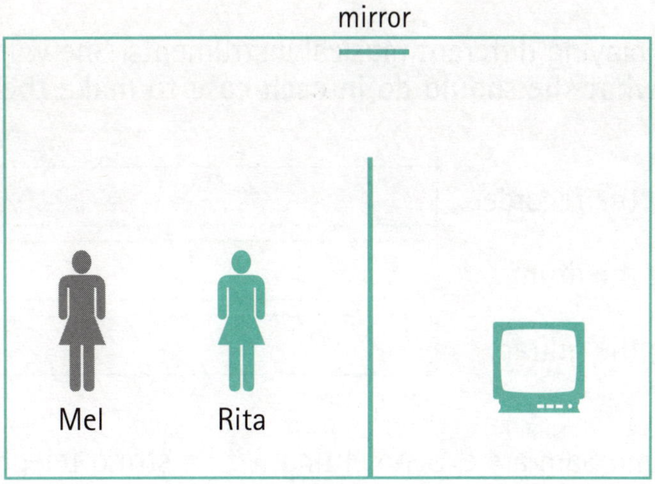

b) Draw in the light from the TV to show how that person sees the reflection.

2 Harry is holding a mirror.
Use arrows to show how he sees the light from the candle.

3 Leah is using two mirrors to see over a crowd.
Use arrows to show how she sees the famous golfer.

Sounds

1 Jade is playing different musical instruments. She wants the sound to be louder.
Write what she should do in each case to make the sound louder.

Playing the recorder

Playing the drum

Playing the guitar

2 Oliver and Sam are experimenting with a string telephone.
Explain how the sound of Sam's voice reaches Oliver when he is listening through the telephone.

3 Hanna listens to Jan tapping on a table top. She can just hear the tap when she is standing next to the table. She can hear the sound better when she has her ear touching the table top.
What does this tell you about the way sound travels through the wood and through air?

4 Faye notices that she can hear sounds better when she cups her hands around her ears.
Explain why this happens.

5 Which of these sentences is most accurate?
Tick the correct box.

Cats have big ears to match the ears of their prey animals. ☐

Cats have big ears so they can run faster. ☐

Cats have big ears because they need good senses for hunting. ☐

Pitch

1 Guitars have strings that can be tightened.

a) What happens to the pitch of a string as it gets tighter?

b) What happens to the pitch of a string as it gets slacker?

2 Drums have screws on the side to make the drum skin tighter and slacker.
Explain how to change the pitch of the sound made by a drum.

a) To make the pitch higher

b) To make the pitch lower

3 a) Which of these tuning forks is likely to make the higher pitched sound?

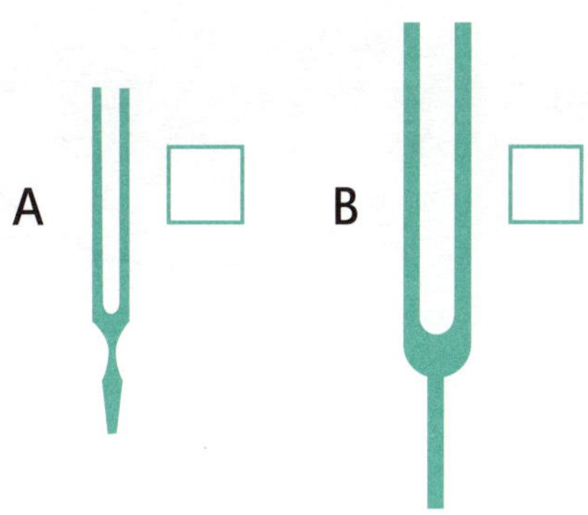

b) Explain your answer.

4 A harp is a musical instrument with long and short strings.

a) Short strings have ______ pitched sounds.

b) Longer strings have ______ pitched sounds.

Movement of the Sun

1 Why does the Sun appear to move across the sky?

2 a) On which horizon does the Sun rise?
Tick the correct box.

North	☐
East	☐
South	☐
West	☐

b) On which horizon does the Sun set?
Tick the correct box.

North	☐
East	☐
South	☐
West	☐

3 This is a view of a globe looking down on the North Pole. The torch represents the Sun.

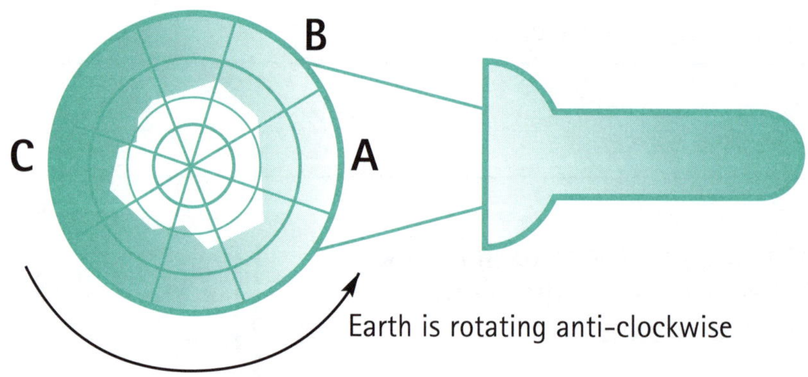

Match the points marked on the globe to the time of day.

	Early morning
A	Midday
B	Midnight
C	Sunrise
	Sunset

The year

1 How many days does it take for the Earth to complete an orbit of the Sun?

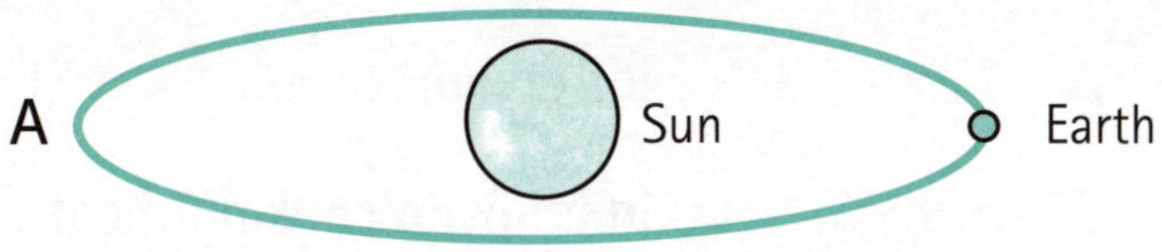

2 How long will it take for the Earth to reach A in its orbit around the Sun?

3 This table shows the approximate time of sunrise in the middle of each month in Britain.

	Jan	Feb	Mar	Apr	May	June	July	Aug	Sept	Oct	Nov	Dec
sunrise a.m.	8.00	7.15	6.15	5.00	4.10	3.45	4.00	4.45	5.35	6.25	7.20	8.00

Harry gets up every school day at 7.30.

a) List the months he gets up before the Sun rises.

b) In which month does the Sun rise earliest in the morning?

c) In which months does the Sun rise latest in the morning?

4 Put a tick next to the sentence that is true.

Sunrise is earlier in the summer. ☐

Sunrise is earlier in the winter. ☐

Sunrise is the same time each day. ☐

Measuring

1 Draw a line from the temperature to the place it was measured.

90 °C	garden on a warm summer day
4 °C	swimming pool
-18 °C	ice cream
0 °C	in an oven cooking meat
22 °C	very hot water
200 °C	inside a freezer
26 °C	inside a fridge

2 This chart shows the results of an experiment.
Kay attached masses to a block of wood. She measured how much mass was needed to move the block on different surfaces.

surface block is on	weight needed to make block move
carpet tile	150 g
smooth paper	55 g
sandpaper	240 g
wooden table top	120 g

a) On which surface was there most friction?

b) On which surface was there least friction?

3 Leo is experimenting with a blue car and a red car rolling down a ramp.
He measures the distance travelled by each car three times.
He finds the average distance for each car.
Why does he do each test three times?

Stretching socks

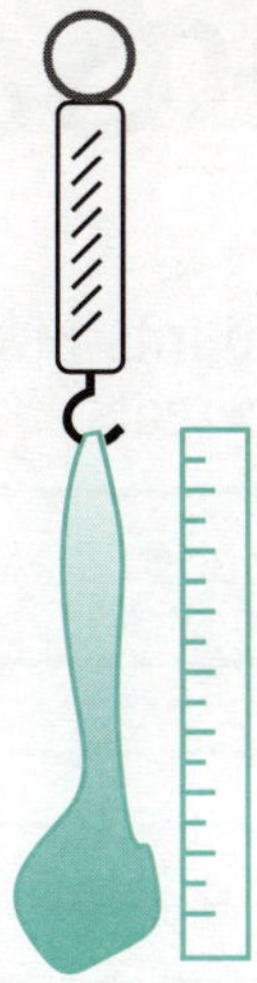

1 Philip puts weights into the toe of an old nylon sock.
He measures the stretch each time.
He keeps on adding weights until he has completed his table.

Mass in sock (grams)	Stretch of sock (cm)
50	3
100	6
150	9
200	12
250	15

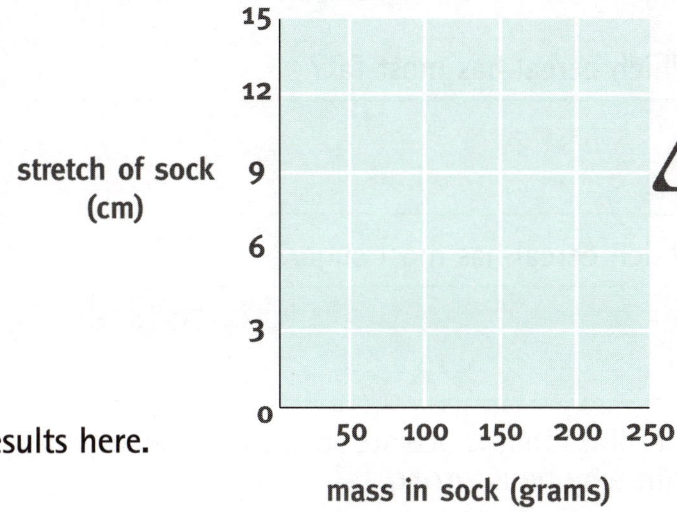

a) Draw a line graph of Philip's results here.

b) What pattern do you notice in the graph?

2 a) Use the graph to work out how much stretch there would be with 75 g mass in the sock. ______ cm stretch of the sock

b) Do you think this pattern will go on for much longer?

c) Explain your answer.

3 Which force is stretching the sock?

Level 4 – Sample test

1 This chart shows the amounts of different food types in breakfast cereals.

	wheat biscuits	cornflakes	cinnamon squares	chocolate squares
protein	11 g	11 g	4 g	10 g
carbohydrate	67 g	82 g	77 g	67 g
of which sugar	5 g	8 g	34 g	32 g
Fat	3 g	1 g	10 g	14 g

a) Which cereal has most fat?

b) Which cereal has most sugar?

c) Jim thinks that chocolate squares are healthy food compared with wheat biscuits. Explain why he is wrong.

2 Flower parts

Label the parts of this flower.

A

B

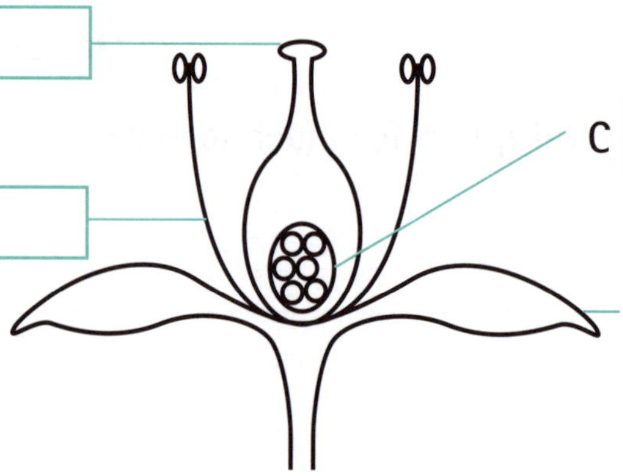

C

D

3 Food chains

Here is a food chain.

sun → grass → rabbit → fox

Underline the producer.

Circle the top predator.

4 Plan an experiment to see how quickly water evaporates from different containers.
Tick the things that are likely to be important in this experiment.

- You start with the same amount of water in each container. ☐
- You have at least three containers with different shapes. ☐
- You keep all the containers in the same place. ☐
- You measure the amount of water you put in each carefully. ☐
- You measure the amount of water left after two days. ☐
- You do the experiment wearing a yellow jumper. ☐
- The same person pours the water in the container. ☐

5 **Which of these materials will dissolve in water? Circle the two that will dissolve.**

salt   sand   sugar   flour

6 **How can you tell when a solid has dissolved in water?**

7 The diagram shows the life cycle of a plant.

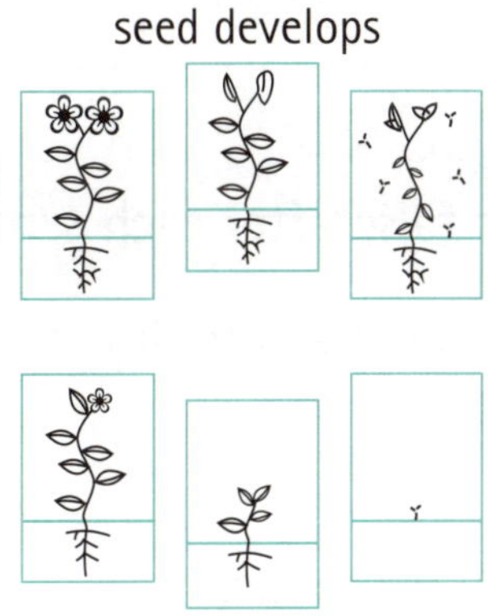

a) What happens when the seed germinates?

b) What two conditions are needed for seeds to germinate?

c) What stage in the life cycle is carried out by bees?

Level 5 – Sample test 1

1 Tom is sitting in a chair writing.

a) Circle two things that will make his heart beat faster.

Underline one thing that will make it beat slower.

running walking drawing resting

b) When his heart beats faster, what is happening to his blood?

material	Does it conduct heat well?	Is it hard?	Does it conduct electricity?	Is it magnetic?
iron	yes	yes	yes	yes
stone	yes	yes	no	no
polystyrene	no	no	no	no
wool	no	no	no	no
aluminium	yes	yes	yes	no

2 Look at the table.

Write true or false after each sentence.

All metals conduct electricity.

All solids are hard.

All metals are magnetic.

3 Gases

Connect the correct gas with its properties.

helium	glows red when electricity passes through it
carbon dioxide	burns
neon	is a very light gas
natural gas	does not burn but will help fires to burn
anaesthetic gas	stops fires from burning and is easily dissolved in water
air	makes you unconscious if you breathe it

4 Forces

a) Show the direction of the force of air resistance on this car.

b) Label these two arrows to show the forces on this floating object.

5 Pitch

In each of these pairs circle the high pitched instrument.
Explain why you think it has the higher pitch.

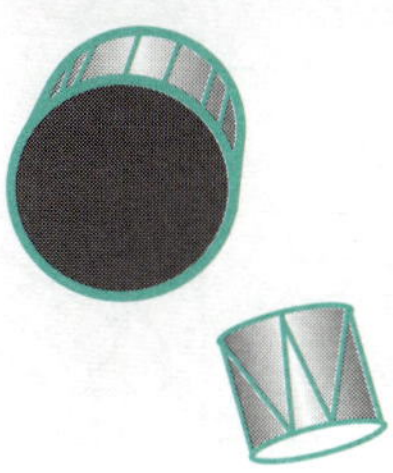

6 Day

Explain why the Sun appears to move across the sky each day.

7 Moon

The Moon orbits the Earth approximately once every 28 days. This is nearly one month.
The lit up part of the moon that is seen from Earth changes during the month.
How long does it take to go from full Moon to half Moon?

Level 5 – Sample test 2

1 a) Which part of a flower produces pollen?

b) Which parts of the flower attract insects?

c) Where are the ovules found in a flower?

2 a) Which part of the human body exchanges gases with the air?

b) Which organ controls the body's movement?

c) Name two functions of the skeleton.

d) Which parts of the body pull bones to make you move?

3 Water changes

Match the description to the correct word.

Water drops form on the inside of a window.	condensation
Liquid water changes to gas.	freeze
Liquid water changes to ice.	evaporation

4 Write down two ways to speed up evaporation from a pan of water.

5

Separate

Write down three steps to separate a mixture of staples, sand and salt.

6

a) Write one way to make a model electric motor turn more quickly.

b) Label the parts of these circuit diagrams.
In these circuits all the bulbs are identical.
Circle the bulbs that will glow most brightly.

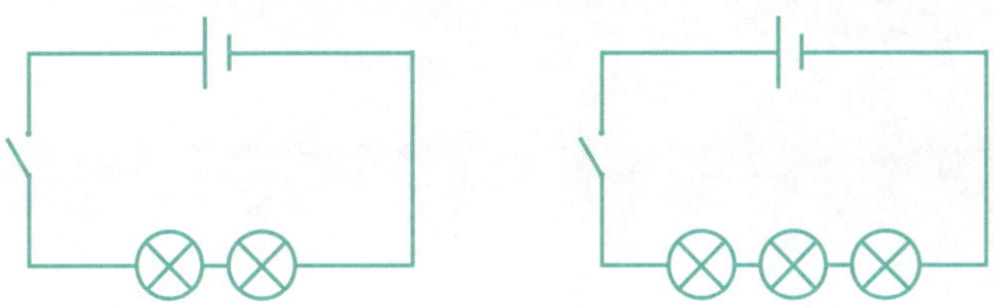

7

Explain how to make the pitch of a drum higher.

8

Explain how the submarine captain can see the ship through this periscope.

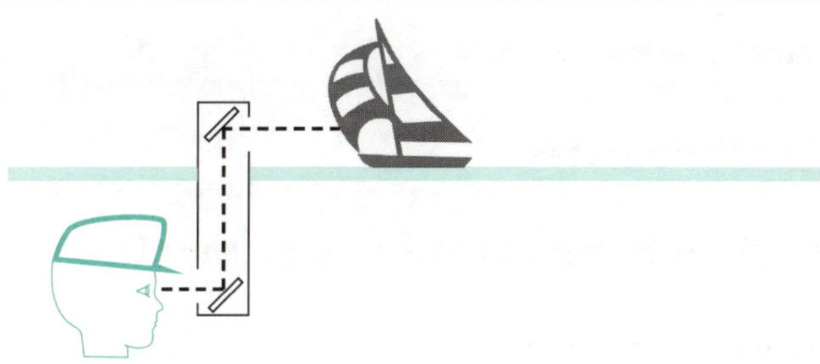

9

a) Laura notices that the shadows made by the Sun start off long in the morning.
They get shorter up to noon.
Explain why this happens.

b) Laura notices that the shadows made by the Sun change direction during the day.
Explain why this happens.

KEY FACTS – Sc1

At Level 4 you need to be able to:

- see that you need evidence to support scientific ideas
- decide on the best way to do an experiment or test
- make good predictions
- select the most important information
- choose the best equipment for a test
- record observations and measurements
- draw and make sense of a bar chart
- come to conclusions
- say ways in which work can be improved

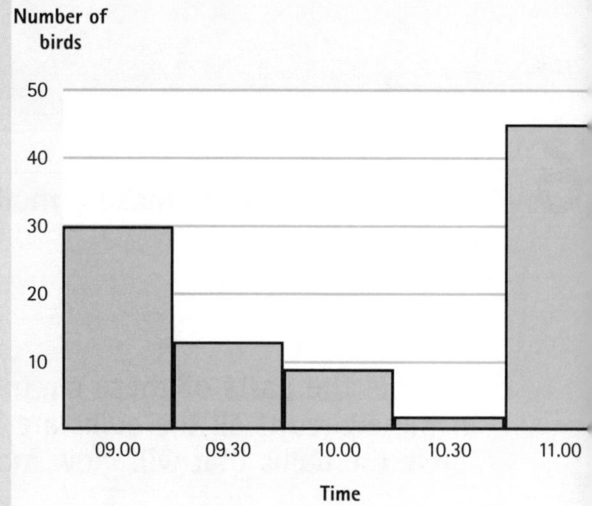

At Level 5 you need to be able to:

- explain scientific ideas
- choose the best information
- choose the right equipment to make measurements
- use the equipment correctly
- repeat measurements
- explain why there might be differences between measurements of the same thing
- understand line graphs
- draw line graphs
- suggest ways in which work could be improved
- use scientific ways to communicate ideas

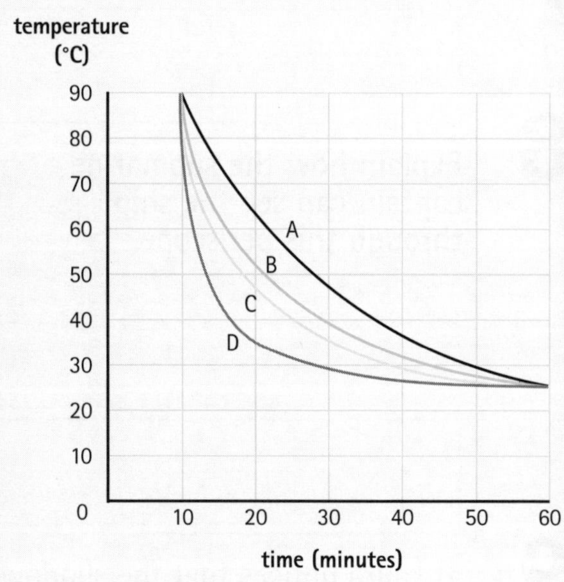

KEY FACTS – Sc2

At Level 4 you need to know:

- the names of some of the organs of the human body
- the position of some of the organs of the human body
- the names and position of some of the organs of a variety of plants
- how to use simple keys to identify living things
- how to put living things into groups
- about food chains

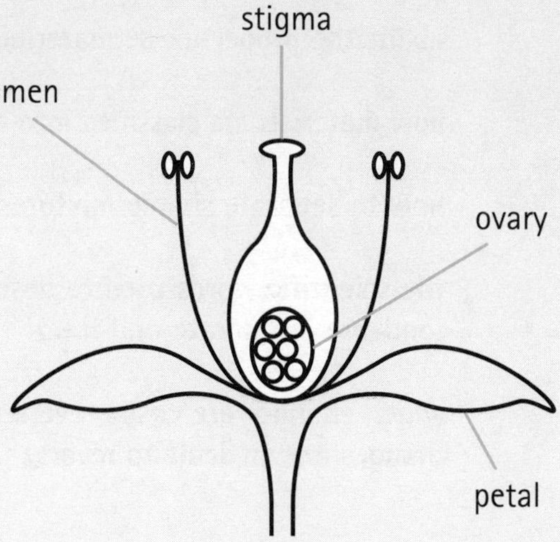

At Level 5 you need to know:

- the jobs done by some of the organs in plants
- about the life cycles of humans and some other animals
- about the life cycles of plants
- how to classify some living things
- that living things are found in places that suit them

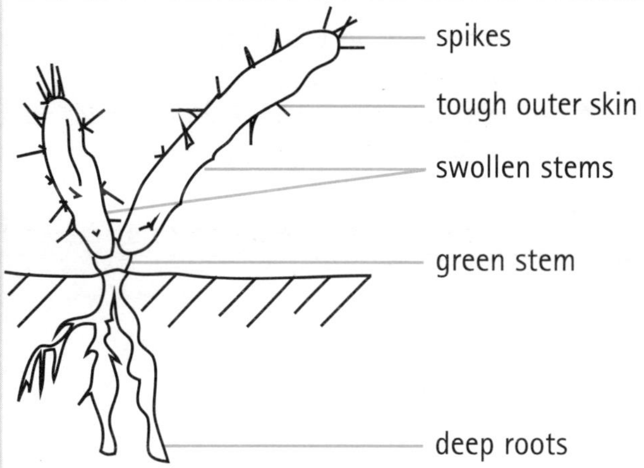

KEY FACTS – Sc3

At Level 4 you need to be able to:

- about the properties of materials
- how materials are classified into solids, liquids and gases
- how to separate simple mixtures
- the scientific words used to describe changes, such as condense, evaporate and freeze
- which changes are easily reversed and which changes are difficult to reverse

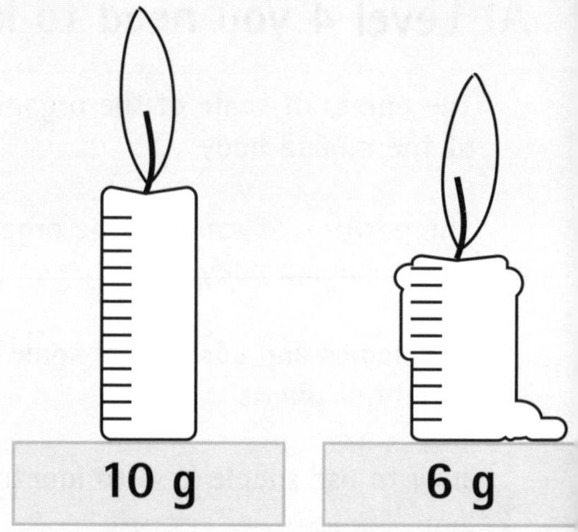

At Level 5 you need to be able to:

- the properties of metals
- the ways in which metals differ from other solids
- the ways in which changes, such as evaporation and condensation, take place
- how to separate mixtures of materials

KEY FACTS – Sc4

At Level 4 you need to know:

- how to alter electrical circuits
- how the Sun changes position during the day
- that objects are attracted by gravity
- which things are attracted by magnets
- that magnets can attract and repel each other
- how shadows are formed
- that sounds travel through a variety of materials

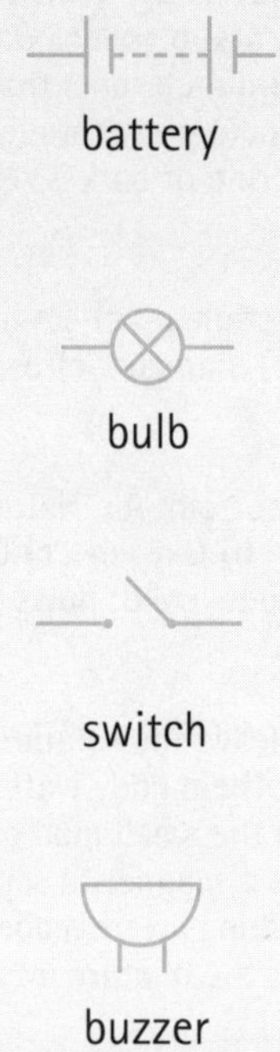

At Level 5 you need to know:

- how to alter the current flowing in a circuit
- about the effect of adding bulbs to a series circuit
- about the effects of adding and subtracting batteries from a circuit
- how to measure forces
- that forces operate in particular directions
- how to draw circuits using symbols
- how to change the pitch and loudness of a sound
- that vibrations result in sounds
- that the light from objects passes into your eyes
- about the orbit of the Earth and the Moon
- how to use knowledge of orbits to explain the length of the day and year

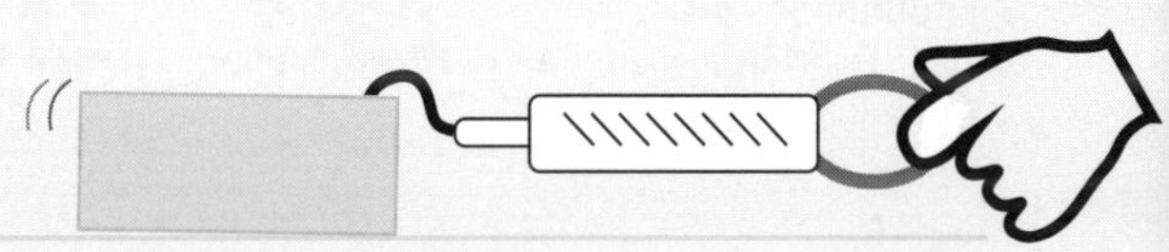

Answers

Page 10
1 Tick: Water travels up stems to leaves; Stems hold the leaves and flowers above the soil.
2 It has deep roots to collect water and a hollow trunk to store water.
3 **a)** They could dig up roots that could bring down trees.
b) The root could grow through the pipes and damage them.
4 Trees die if a ring of bark is removed because it will stop water getting from the roots to the leaves.

Page 11
1 **a)** petal **b)** stigma **c)** stamen **d)** ovary
2 **a)** stigma **b)** stamen **c)** ovary

Page 12
1 From top to bottom: Air, Natural Gas, Carbon Dioxide (from fizzy drink)
2 **a)** Hydrogen **b)** Oxygen **c)** Carbon Dioxide
3 Keeps its shape – solid; flows through a pipe – gas and liquid; can be squashed into a small space – gas

Page 13
1 Matt should leave the solution in a warm place until the water evaporates leaving the sugar.
2 Pat can sieve the muddy water to separate the mud from the water. He may also need to filter the water to remove all the small mud particles.
3 Jim could use a magnet to separate the iron pins from the mixture.
4 If the ball bearings were made of steel, Kate could use a magnet. If the ball bearings were not magnetic, she could put the mixture into water and the polystyrene beads would float.

Page 14
1 **a)** Friction and air resistance
b)

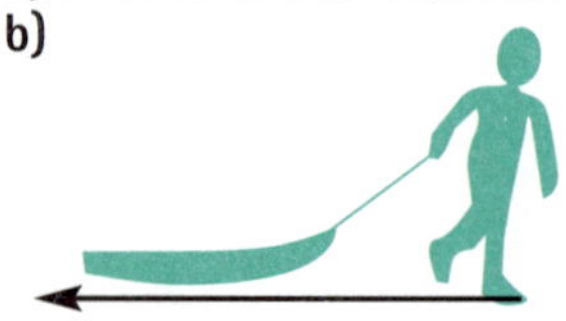

2 Friction
3 Tick: Friction is stopping her from sliding; Friction force is working against gravity.
4 **a)** Gravity **b)** Friction

Page 15
1 **a)** repel **b)** attract **c)** attract **d)** repel
2 Iron or steel
3 **a)** No **b)** Only some metals like iron and steel are magnetic. Others are not magnetic, for example aluminium or copper.
4 Naima can put a magnet under a piece of paper and some iron filings on top. If the iron filings move towards the magnet then the magnetism is passing through the paper.

Page 16
1

Material	magnetic	transparent	opaque	waterproof	conducts electricity
pottery	no	no	yes	yes	no
steel	yes	no	yes	yes	yes
gold	yes	no	yes	yes	yes
window glass	no	yes	no	yes	no
rock	no	no	yes	yes	no

2 **a)** It keeps its shape. **b)** It takes the shape of the bottle and it flows. **c)** I can't see it.
3 Match: sugar to it bubbled and turned black; water to it boiled and evaporated; butter to it melted; salt to nothing happened.
4 rain – liquid, snow – solid, fog – liquid, clouds – liquid, ice – solid

Page 17
1 Tick Which rocks soak up water? Which rocks are hard and which rocks are soft?
2 **a)** He starts by weighing the two rocks. **b)** He soaks the two rocks in water. **c)** He weighs them again and sees which has soaked up the most water.
3 Tim will have to allow the water to evaporate. He could heat the rocks up to help the process.
4 Coal burns.

Page 18
1 **a)** 500 g **b)** 290 g **c)** Tick: first day
2 **a)** The balled rolled further as the ramp got higher. **b)** 65 cm

Page 19
3 **a)** see chart.
b) Human
c) Mouse
d) Lion
e) Mouse
f) Big mammals spend longer inside their mother's body than small ones.
g) Tick: Lions spend more time inside their mother's body than cats; Big mammals spend longer inside their mother's body than small ones; Humans spend longest inside their mother's body so they can develop a big brain.

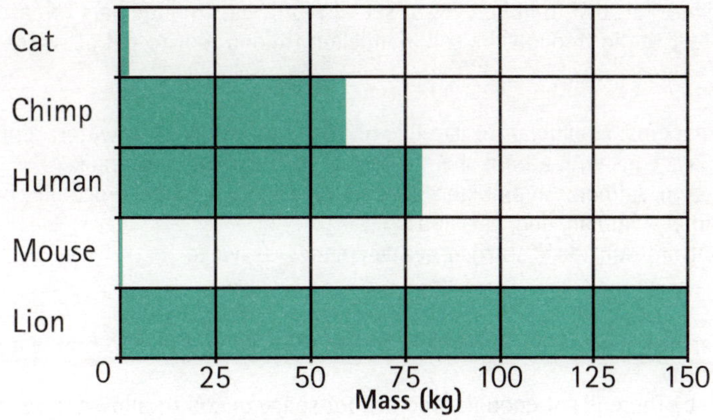

Page 20
1 **a)** Brain **b)** Lungs **c)** Kidneys **d)** Stomach
2 Red on right hand side of diagram, blue on left hand side.
3 Arteries
4 Veins
5 Capillaries

Page 21
1 Oxygen and food
2 Your heart needs to pump faster to get energy to the parts of your body that are exercising.
3 **a)** Chart to read: 80-80-80, 80-110-80, 80-120-80, 80-140-80
b) Jogging requires more energy than walking and less then running fast.
4 Point A – resting, Point B – walking, Point C – running

Page 22
1 **a)** Stigma **b)** Ovary **c)** Stamen
2 To attract insects to the flower. These then pollinate the flower by carrying pollen to the stigma.
3 **a)** Pollen **b)** Nectar
4 Tick: Ovaries are full of ovules; Oak trees only produce acorns if their flowers are pollinated; The stamen produces pollen.

Page 23
1 **a)** Adult butterfly **b)** Eggs **c)** Caterpillar **d)** Pupa
2 **1)** Adults mate **2)** Eggs are laid **3)** Tadpoles hatch **4)** Tadpoles develop legs **5)** New frogs emerge onto the land
3 **1)** Adults mate **2)** Eggs are fertilised by sperm **3)** Baby develops inside the mother **4)** Baby is born **5)** Child grows **6)** Child becomes an adult

Page 24
1 (clockwise from the top) c, e, b, a, d, f
2 Join: apple seeds to eaten by animals such as pigs and carried in droppings; acorns to buried by squirrels and then forgotten; sycamore seeds to blown by the wind; coconut seeds to float in the sea to other islands.
3 To stop overcrowding.
4 Warmth, water, air
5 Light, water, air

Page 25
1 A is polecat; B is pipistrelle
2 From left to right: reptile, amphibian, insect, spider

Page 26
1 Join: cactus to in hot deserts; moss to on walls; reeds to in very damp places; bluebells to under deciduous trees; daisies to in short grass.
2 **a)** Damp paper and lettuce leaves under an upturned box.
b) They have food, they have moisture and a cool environment, they have a dark space to be in.
3 Soil – There is little soil on the wall. Water – There is little water on the wall.

Page 27
1 Streamlined; have feathers to keep them warm; have a beak to grip fish; have short wings, which act as fins in the water.

2 a) white **b)** fur **c)** to catch and eat fish
3 Thorns
4 Prickles
5 Join: antelope to very fast runner and good hearing; lion to very large claws and teeth; camel to humps in which to store fat; owl to huge eyes to see at night; bat to huge ears to catch echoes at night; mole to big front feet to dig through the soil; dandelion to long root to get at water.

Page 28
1 Join: fish to has fins; amphibian to can live on land but lays eggs in water; reptile to has a dry scaly skin; bird to lays eggs with a hard shell; mammal to feeds young on milk.
2 Fish – trout, carp, salmon; Amphibian – frog, toad; Reptile – snake, crocodile; Bird – sparrow, crow, thrush; Mammal – human, dog, cat, lion
3 Top left to bottom right: fish, starfish, sea anemones, seaweed

Page 29
1 a) The one farthest away from the parent. **b)** The roots will be able to find water more easily and it can grow more easily.
2 a) They die. **b)** There is not enough food or root space or soil to allow the seedlings to grow.
3 Because lions do not breed quickly.

Page 30
1

material	**appearance before heating**	**after 20 seconds**	**after 2 minutes**
bread	white, soft, spongy	brown, hard	black, hard, flaky
aluminium foil	shiny, thin, flat	began to curl up and lost shine	lost shine and curled up, glowed red hot

2 Wax, nylon, sugar
3 Plastic, butter, lard, margarine, cheese, chocolate
4 Wax, cotton, nylon, bread, foil
5 Wood, paper, card, string, cloth

Page 31
1 a) Solution **b)** Insoluble
2 You can't see the solid and you have a new liquid.
3 Tick: Using warm water; Stirring the water.
4 a) Amount of crystals, amount of water, temperature of water. **b)** Fine grains **c)** They will dissolve more quickly as each grain is smaller.

Page 32
1 Tick: liquid to gas
2 a) Heat evaporates the water more quickly b) It was the coldest place.
3 a) From top: A, C, B **b)** The gas couldn't escape from jar A because the lid was screwed on.

Page 33
1 Condensation
2 a) Water **b)** Water vapour
3 a) Yes **b)** Some of the water vapour condenses on the pan lid and drips back into the pan.
4 Water vapour from the water is cooled by the ice and turns into droplets on the can.

Page 34
1 From top: melting, evaporation, solidification, condensation
2 The ice melted more quickly when it was warmest.
3 a) –10 °C **b)** 60 minutes **c)** 20 °C

Page 35
1 Sieve the gravy.
2 Allow the water to evaporate.
3 Dissolve the salt in water, then filter out the sand.
4 Iron and paper
5 Wax and sand, polystyrene beads and marbles, wood beads and marbles. Any mixture where one part will sink and the other will float.
6 a) Flour **b)** Salt

Page 36
1
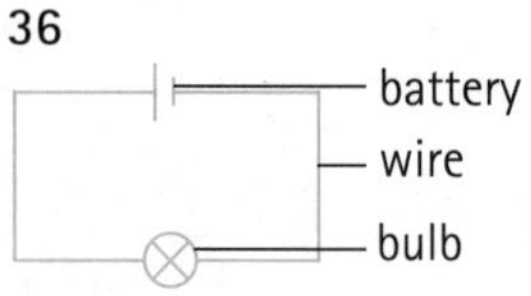

2
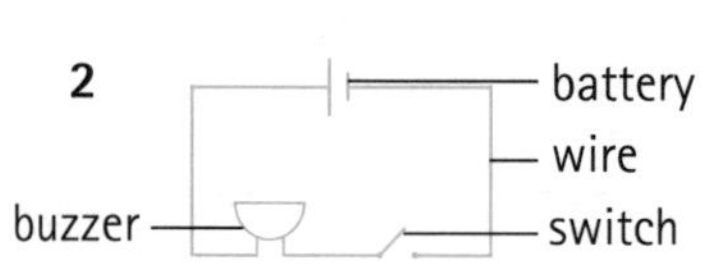

3 The buzzer buzzes. 4 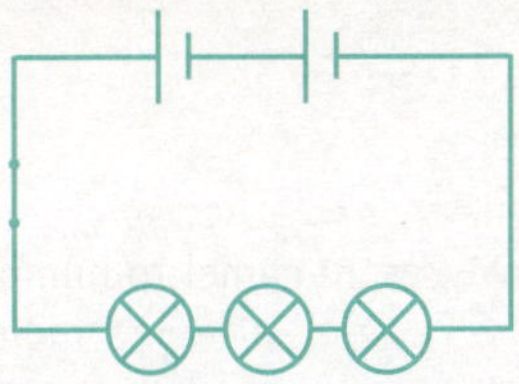

Page 37
1 a) a b) There are 3 batteries, which give more power to the light.
2 c
3 a) The bulb will be dimmer. b) The pencil lead conducts electricity less well than the wire and it has further to go.
4 The pencil will slow down the motor.

Page 38
1 Friction.
2 a) Friction b) Friction; Air resistance
3 Friction and air resistance

Page 39
1 a) 300 g b) 9 N
2 Tick: They will hit the ground at the same time.

Page 40
1 Gravity (arrow down) and Upthrust (arrow up)
2 Sunil
3 There is no air on the Moon, so there is no air resistance.

Page 41
1 Gravity (arrow down) and Upthrust (arrow up)
2 There is more of an upthrust in water.
3 Jamie

Page 42
1 Tick: Move the figure closer to the torch and Move the torch closer to the figure.

2 

3 Tick: A reflection happens when light bounces off something; A shadow happens when light is blocked.

Page 43
1 a) Rita b) 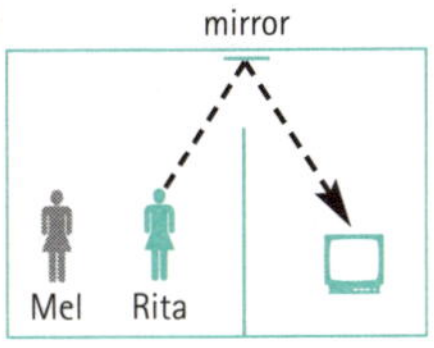

2 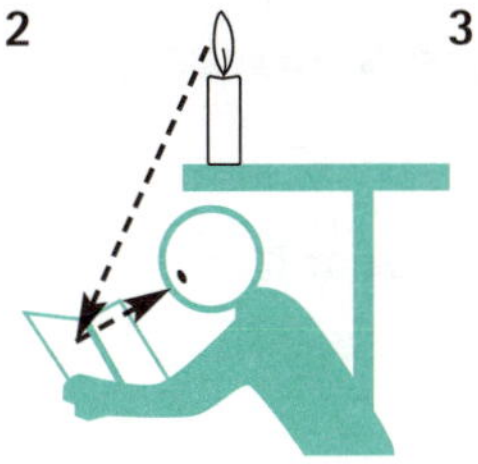
3 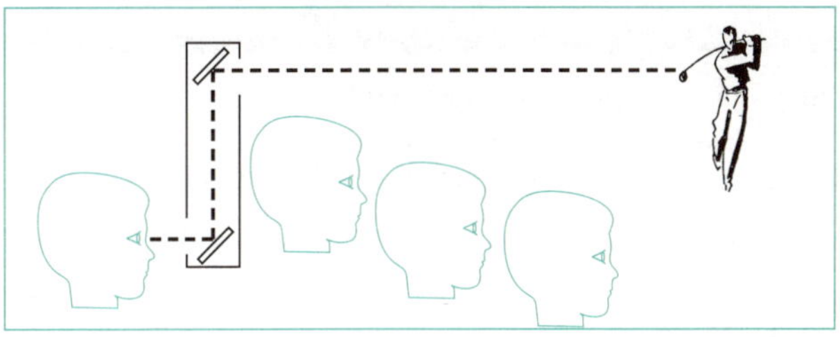

Page 44
1 Blow harder; bang harder; strum harder.
2 The can picks up the vibrations, which are then transmitted through the string to the other can and Oliver's ears.
3 It travels better through wood than air.
4 She catches more of the vibrations with her hand and it funnels more vibrations to her ear.
5 Tick: Cats have big ears because they need good senses for hunting.

Page 45
1 a) Higher b) Lower
2 a) Tighten the skin b) Loosen the skin
3 a) A b) The larger the fork the lower the note
4 a) High b) Low

Page 46
1 The Earth rotates and so the Sun seems to move across the sky when we look at it.
2 a) East b) West
3 A – Midday, B – Sunset, C – Midnight

Page 47
1 $365\frac{1}{4}$ days
2 About 180 days.
3 a) December and January **b)** June **c)** December and January
4 Tick: Sunrise is earlier in the summer.

Page 48
1 Join: 90 °C to very hot water; 4 °C to inside a fridge; –18 °C to inside a freezer; 0 °C to ice cream; 22 °C to garden on a warm summer day; 26 °C to swimming pool; 200 °C to in an oven cooking meat.
2 a) Sandpaper **b)** Smooth paper
3 To ensure he gets the average distance.

Page 49
1 a) Straight line from 0 to top right hand corner of graph. For every 50 grams the sock stretches 3 cm.
b) It is a straight line
2 a) 4.5 cm **b)** No. It will either tear or stop stretching. **c)** Until sock tears.
3 Gravity

Page 50
Level 4 – Sample test
1 a) Chocolate squares **b)** Cinnamon squares **c)** Sugar energy is used up more quickly and too much fat is not good for your arteries.
2 A = Stigma, B = Stamen (or filament), C = Ovary, D = Petal
3 Circle fox and underline grass
4 Tick first 5 boxes
5 Circle salt and sugar
6 The solid is not visible. The solution is clear (transparent).
7 a) The roots grow down, the shoots grow up and leaves begin to form. **b)** Warmth, food **c)** Pollination

Page 52
Level 5 – Sample test 1
1 a) Circle Running and Walking, underline Resting.
b) His blood is being pumped around his body more quickly.
2 a) True **b)** False **c)** False
3 Link: helium to is a very light gas; carbon dioxide to stops first from burning and is easily dissolved in water; neon with glows read when electricity passes through it; natural gas with burns; anaesthetic gas with makes you unconscious if you breathe it; air with does not burn but helps fires to burn.
4 a)

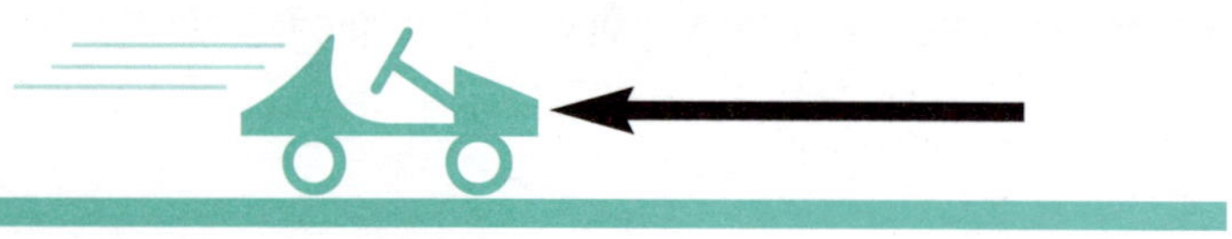

b) Gravity (down arrow), Upthrust (up arrow)
5 Small drum and trumpet have higher pitch.
6 The Earth rotates and so the Sun seems to move across the sky when we look at it.
7 14 days

Page 54
Level 5 – Sample test 2
1 a) Stamen **b)** Petals and nectar **c)** Ovary
2 a) Lungs **b)** Brain **c)** Protects your body parts, lets you move **d)** Muscles
3 Join: Water drops form on the inside of a window to condensation; Liquid water changes to gas to evaporation; Liquid water changes to ice to freeze.
4 To speed up evaporation you should heat the water or put it in a breeze (moving air).
5 Use a magnet to remove the staples, dissolve the salt with water, filter out the sand.
6 a) Add more batteries **b)**

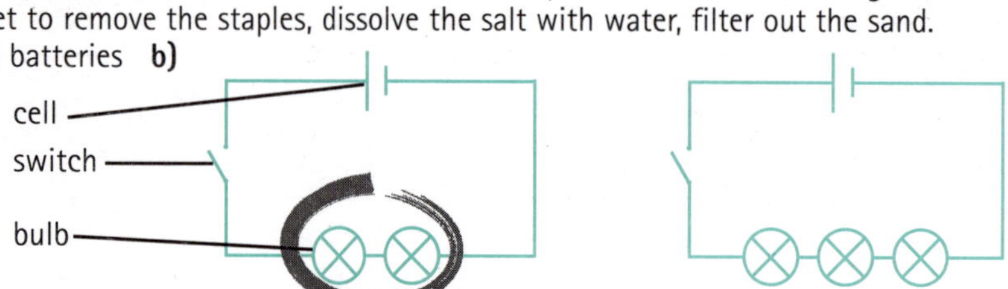

7 Tighten the skin of the drum.
8 Light from the ship goes into the periscope at the top and hits the mirror, which reflects the light down onto a second mirror. This reflects the light into the captain's eye.
9 a) The Sun is low in the sky in the morning and higher up in the sky around noon.
b) As the Earth rotates, the Sun's light comes from a different direction so the shadow seems to move round.